MILTON'S
GRAND STYLE

MILTON'S GRAND STYLE

BY
CHRISTOPHER RICKS

OXFORD
AT THE CLARENDON PRESS
1963

Oxford University Press, Amen House, London E.C.4

GLASGOW NEW YORK TORONTO MELBOURNE WELLINGTON
BOMBAY CALCUTTA MADRAS KARACHI LAHORE DACCA
CAPE TOWN SALISBURY NAIROBI IBADAN ACCRA
KUALA LUMPUR HONG KONG

PRINTED IN GREAT BRITAIN

Prefatory Note

MILTON's Grand Style has been vigorously attacked in the twentieth century, and this book is an attempt to refute Milton's detractors by showing the kind of life which there is in the verse of *Paradise Lost.* Because the style is powerful and grand, it has sometimes been assumed that it is only powerful and grand. I have tried to show its delicacy and subtlety, in the belief that its strength is not that of a steam-roller.

I am very grateful indeed for the advice of those who read an earlier draft: Mr. F. W. Bateson, Mr. John Bryson, Mr. Martin Dodsworth, Mr. John Gross, Mr. Roger Lonsdale, and Mr. W. W. Robson.

For permission to quote, I am grateful to: Mr. T. S. Eliot, and Faber & Faber (*Four Quartets*); Mr. W. H. Auden, and Faber & Faber (*Collected Shorter Poems*); Mr. J. B. Leishman, and the Hogarth Press (R. M. Rilke's *Selected Works*, Volume II); Dr. Donald Davie, and Routledge & Kegan Paul ('Syntax and Music in *Paradise Lost*', in *The Living Milton*, ed. F. Kermode).

C. B. R.

Worcester College, Oxford

Contents

Abbreviations

E. & S.	*Essays and Studies of the English Association*
E. in C.	*Essays in Criticism*
E.L.H.	*E.L.H. A Journal of English Literary History*
O.E.D.	*Oxford English Dictionary*
P.M.L.A.	*Publications of the Modern Language Association of America*

References to Milton's early editors are abbreviated as follows:

Bentley:	Richard Bentley, *Paradise Lost* (1732)
Hume:	Patrick Hume, *Poetical Works of Milton*, *Annotations by P. H.* (1695)
Newton:	Thomas Newton, *Paradise Lost* (1749)
Pearce:	Zachary Pearce, *A Review of the Text of Paradise Lost* (1733)
Richardson:	Jonathan Richardson, Father and Son, *Explanatory Notes on Paradise Lost* (1734)

1. The Milton Controversy

LIKE many years, 1958 saw the publication of a stern letter from Dr. F. R. Leavis. He announced that he was still unwilling to join the conspiracy of silence about Milton, and with much justification he deplored 'the habitual way in which the Miltonists—and the Miltonists command the academic world—virtually ignore the case that has been made against Milton . . . even while they make a show of discussing it'.[1]

Certainly it is true that the twentieth-century attacks on Milton's style have not been directly and satisfactorily answered. Equally certainly, the Miltonists' praise of Milton has not gone very far towards showing what exactly is good about the style of *Paradise Lost*. Perhaps it is natural to feel some impatience about the whole matter. Even Professor William Empson saw nothing evasive in saying 'I can sympathize with a critic who feels he cannot take seriously a proof that the poem is bad—it is so evidently not bad'.[2] But if, as Dr. Johnson thought, it is the duty of criticism to 'improve opinion into knowledge', then it is hard to be satisfied with opinion. Moreover, Milton's style is still an interesting challenge to the verbal criticism which now seems one of the most important and useful ways of approaching literature.

Milton, then, can provoke a crisis of conscience. Is it possible to reconcile one's honest opinion that *Paradise Lost* is supremely well written with one's opinion that verbal

[1] *The Times Literary Supplement*, 19 Sept. 1958.

[2] *T.L.S.*, 3 Oct. 1958.

criticism is usually a just judge? Has Dr. Leavis really provided what Mr. Empson dryly calls 'a proof that the poem is bad'? Has Dr. Leavis 'so convincingly denied' to Milton's style 'the qualities of sensitivity and subtlety'?[1]

The traditionalists need feel no difficulty. Professor F. T. Prince has referred to 'the fact that Milton's poetry does not respond to this kind of analysis and appreciation [New Criticism], and that his work has therefore always been ranked low by the founders and followers of this school'.[2] But is it a *fact* that Milton's poetry doesn't respond to New Criticism? It is certainly the opposite of a fact that Milton has always been ranked low by such critics. Mr. Empson? Mr. Cleanth Brooks?

Yet it is the anti-Miltonists who have provided what is, in some ways, the most useful approach to Milton. Not, I think, that their criticisms are true, but in taking seriously Milton's use of words, they force the same kind of seriousness on their opponents. From Dr. Leavis and Mr. T. S. Eliot—the foremost though not the only modern anti-Miltonists[3]—one can perhaps construct a positive understanding of Milton's style. The grittiness of their method may one day produce a pearl.

Dr. Leavis's essay on 'Milton's Verse' was originally published as an article in *Scrutiny* in 1933, though it did not appear in book-form (in *Revaluation*) till 1936. So it precedes Mr. Eliot's full-length piece. Dr. Leavis attacked 'the inescapable monotony of the ritual', insisting that 'the pattern, the stylized gesture and movement, has no particular expressive work to do, but functions by rote, of its own momentum, in the manner of a ritual'. 'To say that Milton's verse is magniloquent', he urged, 'is to say that it is not doing as much as its impressive pomp and volume seem to be asserting; that mere orotundity is a disproportionate part of the

[1] Bernard Bergonzi, in *The Living Milton* (ed. F. Kermode, 1960), p. 174.

[2] 'On the Last Two Books of *P.L.*', *E. & S.* (1958), p. 47.

[3] Eliot had made many potent asides about Milton before his essay of 1936. Other influential anti-Miltonists were Ezra Pound, Middleton Murry, and Herbert Read.

whole effect; and that it demands more deference than it merits.' And he condemned the Grand Style: 'It needs no unusual sensitiveness to language to perceive that, in this Grand Style, the medium calls pervasively for a kind of attention, compels an attitude towards itself, that is incompatible with sharp, concrete realization.' For the Grand Style is responsible for 'the extreme and consistent remoteness of Milton's medium from any English that was ever spoken'. Indeed, 'cultivating so complete and systematic a callousness to the intrinsic nature of English, Milton forfeits all possibility of subtle or delicate life in his verse'. Dr. Leavis quoted an excellent passage of Donne, and added: 'This is the Shakespearian use of English; one might say that it is the English use.' In Milton, on the other hand, 'certain feelings are expressed, but there is no pressure behind the words; what predominates in the handling of them is not the tension of something precise to be defined and fixed, but a concern for mellifluousness—for liquid sequences and a pleasing opening and closing of the vowels'.[1]

In studying Dr. Leavis's argument, one must first notice that he is not above a pretty blatant bullying: 'It should be obvious at once to any one capable of being convinced at all . . . '; or 'It would be of no use to try and argue with any one who contended that . . .'; or 'It needs no unusual sensitiveness to language to perceive that . . .'. It is important that we should not just knuckle under. But it is also important that we shouldn't assume that bullying necessarily conceals poor arguments.

The second point is larger: 'the Shakespearian use of English'. Dr. Leavis has always insisted on this 'exploratory-creative use of words'—what Mr. Eliot called 'that perpetual slight alteration of language, words perpetually juxtaposed in new and sudden combinations, meanings perpetually *eingeschachtelt* into meanings'.[2] And in contrasting Donne with Milton, Dr. Leavis relied on this criterion:

[1] *Revaluation* (1936), pp. 42–61.

[2] 'Philip Massinger' (1920), *Selected Essays* (2nd ed., 1934), p. 209.

Donne's 'is the Shakespearian use of English; one might say that it is the English use'. In that case, what of Dr. Leavis's own praise of *The Vanity of Human Wishes*: 'This is great poetry, though unlike anything that this description readily suggests to modern taste; it is a poetry of statement, exposition and reflection: nothing could be remoter from the Shakespearean use of language—"In this passage is exerted all the force of poetry, that force which calls new powers into being, which embodies sentiment, and animates matter"—than the Johnsonian.'[1] But if Johnson's poetry can be great and yet as remote as possible from the Shakespearian use of language, why can't Milton's too?

Not that this inconsistency is just a chance to crow over Dr. Leavis. On the contrary, it is one of the best examples of the honesty of his criticism. Really feeling the greatness of Johnson's poetry, he is prepared to admit the limitations of the criterion to which he usually clings so closely. Matthew Arnold, with great passion, praises a similar moment in Burke's writing:

> That return of Burke upon himself has always seemed to me one of the finest things in English literature, or indeed in any literature. That is what I call living by ideas: when one side of a question has long had your earnest support, when all your feelings are engaged, when you hear all round you no language but one, when your party talks this language like a steam-engine and can imagine no other,—still to be able to think, still to be irresistibly carried, if so it be, by the current of thought to the opposite side of the question.[2]

And oddly enough, there is a very similar moment in Johnson's criticism of Milton.[3] At considerable length he explains why blank verse is inferior to the heroic couplet, and then with an engaging *volte-face* he admits: 'Whatever be the advantage of rhyme I cannot prevail on myself to wish that Milton had been a rhymer.' Certainly the inability to prevail on oneself is a mark of the notable critic. Yet to give Dr.

[1] 'Johnson as Poet' (1942), *The Common Pursuit* (1952), p. 118.

[2] 'The Function of Criticism at the Present Time.'

[3] *Lives of the Poets*, ed. G. B. Hill (1905), i. 194.

Leavis such credit is not to forget his inconsistency on the crucial question of the Shakespearian use of language.

But these immediate points give way to a more important one—that Dr. Leavis has accepted the traditional opinion of Milton's style, and then presented it as exactly what is wrong with the poetry. It is this above all which has left the traditionalist defenders of Milton either weakly silent or else confined to skirmishes on the edges of the argument. As Charles Williams wittily pointed out, 'the orthodox Chairs of Literature, it must be admitted, had for long professed the traditional view of an august, solemn, proud, and (on the whole) unintelligent and uninteresting Milton'. What had been said with admiration was now said with contempt: 'the solemn rituals in praise of Milton were suddenly profaned by a change of accent, but the choruses had not altered; what then were the pious worshippers to do?'[1]

The 'pious worshippers' had to contend not only with Dr. Leavis but with Mr. Eliot, whose first essay on Milton[2] was published in 1936. (A great deal of it, as of the second essay, is concerned with Milton's influence, which is hardly a matter of literary criticism but belongs to the literary historian or the historian of ideas.) Mr. Eliot's argument was, in essence, the same as Dr. Leavis's: in Milton, 'the arrangement [of words] is for the sake of musical value, not for significance'. And 'the syntax is determined by the musical significance, by the auditory imagination, rather than by the attempt to follow actual speech or thought'. The result is often something which 'is not serious poetry, not poetry fully occupied about its business, but rather a solemn game'.[3]

Mr. Eliot's second piece, his British Academy lecture of 1947, is often seen as the return of the prodigal. But it is not exactly a recantation; Mr. Eliot still sees in Milton what he saw before. True, he now sees it as worthy of praise instead of blame, but the praise is quite exceptionally feline, even for

[1] Introduction to *The English Poems of Milton* (World's Classics, 1940), pp. ix, xi.

[2] *E. & S.*, xxi (which is for 1935, though the title-page is dated 1936).

[3] 'Milton I.' *On Poetry and Poets* (1957), pp. 142, 144.

Mr. Eliot. Take, for example, his equilibrist admiration for 'Milton's skill in extending a period by introducing imagery which tends to distract us from the real subject'.

It is with the same delicacy that he befriends Milton's comparison of Satan to a leviathan upon which seamen mistakenly moor:

> What I wish to call to your attention is the happy introduction of so much extraneous matter. Any writer, straining for images of hugeness, might have thought of the whale, but only Milton could have included the anecdote of the deluded seamen without our wanting to put a blue pencil through it. We *nearly* forget Satan in attending to the story of the whale; Milton recalls us just in time.[1]

This demands two comments. The first is to insist on the way in which such praise trembles on the edge of blame. The second is to insist that Mr. Eliot has his facts wrong. Satan was traditionally compared to a whale upon which trusting man moored.[2] So the simile is prophetic of the Fall. And far from its being 'only Milton' who could have brought in such a story without our wanting to strike it out, very many others could have done so. Of course, we can then turn the whole attack round, and accuse Milton of being stale. But that was not what Mr. Eliot wished to call to our attention.

Hardly a recantation, then. After all, to praise the 'inspired frivolity' of a religious epic—even when we allow for 'If I may put it in this way without being misunderstood'—is deliberately to leave open all sorts of cunning passages from praise to blame. The whole essay is a fine example of an evasiveness in Mr. Eliot which is so strong as to become almost a mark of greatness—though the greatness is that of Houdini. As Mr. Yvor Winters has said, 'at any given time he can speak with equal firmness and dignity on both sides of

[1] *Proceedings of the British Academy* (1947), xxxiii. 74–75. Omitted from 'Milton II', *On Poetry and Poets.*

[2] The tradition is widespread in the Bestiaries and elsewhere, and the evidence has been assembled by, among others, James Whaler (*P.M.L.A.* 1931, xlvi. 1050); Rosemary Freeman (*English Emblem Books*, 1948, p. 92); K. Svendsen (*Milton and Science*, 1956, pp. 33–35); and D. M. Hill (*Notes and Queries*, April 1956, p. 158). I return to Milton's similes in Chapter 4.

almost any question'. And unfortunately the original lecture has been severely cut for its appearance in *On Poetry and Poets*. The quotations from Milton have disappeared, and so have the good words which Mr. Eliot put in for them.

Meanwhile Dr. Leavis had written on 'Mr. Eliot and Milton'. His aim was to show that Mr. Eliot's strictures were far more convincing than his bland suggestion that all was really for the best. When, for example, Mr. Eliot sighs about inconsistency, Dr. Leavis acts as an amplifier: 'These criticisms seem to me unanswerable, though, properly understood, they amount to more than criticism of mere detail—unanswerable, unless with the argument that if you read Milton as he demands to be read you see no occasion to make them.' Even when Milton is at his best, Dr. Leavis argues, 'there is no sharp challenge to a critical or realizing awareness—there is the relaxation of the demand for consistency characteristic of rhetoric'. There is a 'looseness about meaning', and 'we are happy about the introduction of so much extraneous matter because the "Miltonic music" weakens our sense of relevance, just as it relaxes our grasp of sense'. And in a final desperate footnote, convinced that all his arguments have made no headway in the academic world, Dr. Leavis cries out that 'Milton has been made the keep of an anti-critical defensive system'.[1]

The basic point of the anti-Miltonists, then, is simply that Milton's poetry doesn't *mean* very much, that the verbal music thrives at the expense of—instead of in harmony with—any precise relevance. Milton is evidently intoxicating, but is intoxication the proper pleasure of poetry? In Shakespeare, in Donne, in Pope (they might argue), exhilaration is compatible with precision and sense. And moreover the *words* of such poets are not static and fixed in their meanings, but are exploratory and creative, in 'that perpetual slight alteration of language'. These charges could hardly be more important, and to consider them may advance an understanding of exactly what Milton's poetry is.

[1] *The Common Pursuit*, pp. 15, 19 n., 22, 32 n.

The most lively and influential of the traditionalists is Professor C. S. Lewis. Unfortunately for the literary critic, Mr. Lewis hands the argument over at once to the philosopher and the theologian:

> I have already noted this peculiar difficulty in meeting the adverse critics, that they blame it for the very qualities which Milton and his lovers regard as virtues. . . . Dr. Leavis does not differ from me about the properties of Milton's epic verse. He describes them very accurately—and understands them better, in my opinion, than Mr. Pearsall Smith [who had attempted a reply to Dr. Leavis]. It is not that he and I see different things when we look at *Paradise Lost*. He sees and hates the very same that I see and love. Hence the disagreement between us tends to escape from the realm of literary criticism. We differ not about the nature of Milton's poetry, but about the nature of man, or even the nature of joy itself.[1]

The extent of the split can be seen when Mr. Lewis approves of Goethe's description of 'the epic diction' as 'a language which does your thinking and your poetizing for you'[2]—a point of view totally opposed to that of Dr. Leavis. And faced with such a divergence, we may well wonder whether there is anything for it but to look at our fundamental principles, see whether they align us with Leavis or Lewis, and then take up the appropriate stance. Mr. Bernard Bergonzi, for example, believes that the anti-Miltonists' terms of reference are wrong or too narrow, but claims that, within these terms, they are unanswerable: 'Leavis . . . might be satisfied by an opponent who tries to show that Milton's Grand Style *did* possess the qualities of sensitivity and subtlety and expressive closeness to the movements of actual sensory experience that Leavis has so convincingly denied to it; but not otherwise. And it is most unlikely that anyone would be found to make the attempt.'[3]

But there is a third point of view which does just this, one represented by such critics as William Empson, Cleanth Brooks, and J. B. Broadbent. They seem to me in some sense

[1] *A Preface to P.L.* (1942), pp. 129–30. [2] p. 23.

[3] 'Criticism and the Milton Controversy', *The Living Milton*, p. 174.

to share Dr. Leavis's view of what poetry should be, but they believe that Milton's poetry accords with it. That it *is* sensitive and subtle. That Milton *does* make use of expressive closeness to the senses when the occasion demands. That his words are not sealed off as if they were in cellophane bags. And that our standards of relevance and consistency must be as sharp as usual. Such critics might say, perhaps, not that Dr. Leavis's *principles* are wrong, but that his *tools* are few and inadequate.

My own preference is for this position. To me, Milton is a great poet; but likewise, the criteria of meaning, precision, and creative language seem essentially apt. Apt, surely, at the level of Milton's achievement, comparable as it is to Shakespeare and Dante. Milton himself would presumably have preferred (if it were coherently argued) a harsh judgement by a standard that is itself a compliment, rather than the condescending view represented by that sentence of Goethe. Milton must surely have felt that he did his thinking and poetizing for himself. And he was contemptuous of the opponent who 'insists upon the old Plea of *his Conscience, honour, and Reason*; using the plausibility of large and indefinite words, to defend himself at such a distance as may hinder the eye of common judgement from all distinct view & examination of his reasoning'.[1]

The best document for this third critical position is Mr. Empson's exciting and provocative chapter in *Some Versions of Pastoral* (1935). He took as his starting-point the extraordinary edition of *Paradise Lost* published in 1732 by Richard Bentley, the great classical scholar. Bentley was convinced that the text was hopelessly corrupt, and so introduced drastic emendations wherever his rigid rationality suggested. (In 1733 many of his points were answered in the same terms by Zachary Pearce.) Mr. Empson saw that Bentley's famous failure

scared later English critics into an anxiety to show that they were sympathetic and did not mind about the sense. One has only to compare

[1] *Eikonoklastes*, XI.

such duellists as Pearce and Bentley, who raise questions at every point, however they fail to answer them, which concern the essence of the poetry they are considering, with the mild and tactful hints, the air of a waiter anxious not to interrupt the conversation, of a sensible nineteenth-century editor like Masson.[1]

It was brilliantly acute of Mr. Empson to fasten on the early editors as providing a precedent for his own subtly imaginative reading of Milton. Yet provocative and valuable though Bentley is, it is misleading to give a central position to one who is incorrigibly eccentric. Bentley, as Mr. Empson has shown, can again and again provide a stimulus; but for quieter virtues we must make full use of the other early editors. There is P. H. (Patrick Hume), whose *Annotations on Paradise Lost* were published in 1695, only twenty-one years after Milton's death. There is 'Jonathan Richardson, Father and Son', whose *Explanatory Notes* on *Paradise Lost* (1734) may not always explain but often suggest. And there is Thomas Newton, whose variorum edition of *Paradise Lost* (1749) draws on these and many other commentators with much skill and subtlety. In discussing the Milton controversy, we may think of such editors as holding the third position that I have outlined, and which Mr. Empson may be said to represent today.

The Milton controversy, then, is triangular. Leavis and Lewis agree as to what the poem is, but differ as to what a poem should be, and so as to how good it is. Leavis and (say) Empson agree as to what a poem should be, but differ as to what the poem is, and so as to how good it is. Meanwhile Lewis and Empson agree as to how good the poem is, but differ about what it is and what a poem should be.

To meet the anti-Miltonists' case as it should be met, it is best to take a passage where an objection by Mr. Eliot was endorsed by Dr. Leavis. In the council in Hell, Moloch advocates open war:

[1] *Some Versions of Pastoral* (1935), p. 152.

> My sentence is for open Warr: Of Wiles,
> More unexpert, I boast not: them let those
> Contrive who need, or when they need, not now.
> For while they sit contriving, shall the rest,
> Millions that stand in Arms, and longing wait
> The Signal to ascend, sit lingring here
> Heav'ns fugitives . . . (II. 51–57)

Mr. Eliot murmured that 'it might, of course, be objected that "millions that *stand* in arms" could not at the same time "*sit* lingring" '.[1] And Dr. Leavis seized on this example to insist that 'there is no sharp challenge to a critical or realizing awareness—there is the relaxation of the demand for consistency characteristic of rhetoric'.[2]

It is easy enough to guess two of the traditionalist defences that might be put forward. First, that stand in arms does not mean *stand* but merely *be* in arms—whereupon the use of stand in a Latinate way can be demonstrated elsewhere in the poem. The snag about so schoolmasterly a defence would be that, in clearing Milton of the charge of inconsistency, it immediately lays him open to a far worse one: that of being so insensitive to words that he uses *sit* in one line, *stand* in the next, and *sit* in the third, and apparently doesn't realize that the two *sit*'s will exert a pressure on the word 'stand', making us want to take it literally. The schoolmaster plays straight into Dr. Leavis's hands.

So does another conceivable academic defence: that to complain about such an inconsistency is merely to niggle, that we are swept along by the grand majestic flow, the Miltonic music, the epic style. Exactly, would retort the anti-Miltonists, when you stop and look at it, it's muddled. Its effect depends on a confidence trick, on what Milton himself deplored as 'the plausibility of large and indefinite words'.

But is it possible to accept the demand for consistency and still defend Milton here? Of course. Mr. Eliot's slip (and Dr. Leavis's) is in objecting that 'millions that stand in arms

[1] *Proceedings of the British Academy* (1947), xxxiii. 76 n.
[2] *The Common Pursuit*, p. 19 n.

could not *at the same time* sit lingring'. They could not, but Milton doesn't say they could. He has a future and a present tense:

> *shall* the rest,
> Millions that stand in Arms, and longing wait
> The Signal to ascend, sit lingring here . . .[1]

There is no inconsistency here, there is a deliberate clash. Moloch begins (without any 'Ladies and Gentlemen', or the 'O Peers' of Belial) with a bluntly *open* and straightforward voice: 'My sentence is for open Warr.' We can see how fatal any suggestion of indirection would be here when Dryden, in *The State of Innocence*, rewrites the line as 'My sentence is for War; that open too'.[2]

Moloch's syntax then becomes circuitous, not because Milton is trying to elevate his native tongue, or because he has a habit of Latinizing, but because the circuitousness is to ridicule the devious people who hold a different point of view from fiercely direct Moloch:

> Of Wiles,
> More unexpert, I boast not: them let those
> Contrive who need, or when they need, not now.

The openness of open war is clashed against the roundabout wiles of military planners; and the manipulation of ordinary syntax brings *Wiles* hard up against its alliterating monosyllable *Warr*, so that the manly fortitude of the one blasts the procrastination of the other. 'I boast not' is a boast; as who should say 'Of course I don't know anything about manœuvres, I've only been in the front line for the last eighteen months'. It is just this traditional antagonism which Moloch plays on.

Planners need to *contrive*; and Moloch toys with the word again contemptuously, tossing in the equally contemptuous *sit*: 'For while they sit contriving, shall the rest . . .'. At which, he brilliantly numbers those that are of his way of

[1] My italics here and throughout in quotations from Milton's poems (which are from H. C. Beeching's reprint, 1900). I have removed the italics from proper names.

[2] 1677. Act I.

thinking (and acting), and contrasts their military stance with the sitting-about of the not-numbered 'they':

> shall the rest,
> Millions that stand in Arms, and longing wait
> The Signal to ascend . . .

And at that dramatic point, the superb upward thrust of *sit*, *stand*, *ascend* is razed by the deliberate bathos of *sit* again:

> Millions that stand in Arms, and longing wait
> The Signal to ascend, sit lingring here . . .

The contrivers (the Belials) want to turn standers into sitters. And with fighting skill, Moloch answers the participle in 'sit contriving' with the same construction in 'sit lingring'. Men who stand will be made to sit. Men who long will be made to linger, as the echo from the previous line (longing/lingring) reminds us.

'Does this make sense?' asked Milton's judges, but did not stay for an answer. Yet without their question, it may be that we would not have noticed exactly what was being said. And when the crank Charles Eyre rewrote the lines in 1852, his version brought out just how powerful were the words he omitted—*contrive*, for one, but above all the placing of *stand* and *sit*:

> My sentence is for open war; of wiles
> More inexpert I boast not; them let those
> Invent who need—and when there 's need—not now.
> For while they sit contriving, shall the rest,
> Millions in arms, who with impatience wait
> The signal to ascend, here lingering stand,
> Heaven's fugitives . . .[1]

This particular example, though, can make two points. One, that the anti-Miltonists haven't always been careful enough. The other, that the eighteenth-century editors are still in many ways the best guide to Milton. In fact, the whole argument had been thrashed out two hundred years

[1] *The Fall of Adam* (1852), p. 17.

before Mr. Eliot and Dr. Leavis. Bentley in 1732 had growled: 'Observe the Inconsistence, *Stand* in Arms *sit* ling'ring. No doubt therefore he gave it, STAY *ling'ring here*.'[1] Pearce in 1733 took refuge in the schoolmasterly: '*stand* does not always signify the posture . . . *stand in Arms*, signifies *are in Arms*'.[2] And he was supported by Jonathan Richardson in 1734: '*Stand and Sit* are Metaphorical, and no Contradiction therefore; Stand, as being Prepar'd, and Sit, as Idly Lingering.'[3] But what is surely the true meaning was seen in 1749 by Thomas Newton, who made his point with admirable brevity: '*Sit ling'ring* to answer *sit contriving* before. While they sit contriving, shall the rest sit ling'ring?'[4]

The eighteenth-century arguments about Milton are in many ways a mirror of the modern one. Bentley, like the anti-Miltonists, had a great gift for getting hold of the right thing—by the wrong end. Again and again he sees exactly what is happening in a passage of Milton. He then deplores it, but we need not do so, and can be grateful for his insight. He may be wrong-headed, but at least he is headed.

He is particularly quick to spot the kind of clash which Milton is so fond of and which is not carelessness.

> Uplifted imminent one stroke they aim'd. (VI. 317)

'*Uplifted* and *Imminent* contradict each other: for *Uplifted* has a Motion upwards, and *Imminent* a tendence downwards.'[5] Bentley is right about how the style works here, but wrong about its value, as Pearce insisted: '*Uplifted* is what has *had* a Motion upwards, but has that Motion no longer, when it is already *uplifted*: and *imminent* is what hovers and is ready to fall, but has not as yet in the least begun to do so. In these two Senses the two words may meet very lovingly together.'[6] Yet, as Miss Darbishire remarked, 'Such interrogations not only stamp Bentley's failure in poetic imagination, they also awaken us to a boldness, a violence, a tendency to paradox in Milton's

[1] *P.L.* (1732), p. 38.

[2] *A Review of the Text of P.L.* (1733), pp. 50, 359.

[3] *Explanatory Notes on P.L.*, J. Richardson, Father and Son (1734), p. 52.

[4] *P.L.* (1749), i. 84. [5] p. 193. [6] p. 211.

imaginative phrasing which the splendour and sustained majesty of his style in *Paradise Lost* tend to mask.'[1]

Similarly Bentley notices the contradictions in the presentation of the fallen angels, but fails to see how they are part of Milton's purpose. Moloch remembers

> With what compulsion and laborious flight
> We sunk thus low . . . (II. 80–81)

'The Ideas of *Flight* and of *Sinking* do not agree well together.'[2] Indeed they don't—that is just the point. Any more than the words *fallen* and *angel* agree well together. But it was for De Quincey to explain the principles involved:

> Each image, from reciprocal contradiction, brightens and vivifies the other. The two images act, and react, by strong repulsion and antagonism. . . . Out of this one principle of subtle and lurking antagonism, may be explained everything which has been denounced under the idea of pedantry in Milton. . . . For instance, this is the key to that image in the 'Paradise Regained', where Satan, on first emerging into sight, is compared to an old man gathering sticks, 'to warm him on a winter's day'. This image, at first sight, seems little in harmony with the wild and awful character of the supreme fiend. No; it is *not in* harmony, nor is it meant to be in harmony. On the contrary, it is meant to be in antagonism and intense repulsion. The household image of old age, of human infirmity, and of domestic hearths, are all meant as a machinery for provoking and soliciting the fearful idea to which they are placed in collision, and as so many repelling poles.[3]

With his usual mistaken acuteness, Bentley brings out the superbly contemptuous pun when the devils shrink:

> Thus incorporeal Spirits to smallest forms
> Reduc'd thir shapes immense, and were at large . . . (I. 789–90)

'By being *at large*, the Author means, *being not crouded*. . . . But here it's shocking at first Reading: contracting their Shapes to the *smallest* Size, and yet being *at large*.'[4] Certainly it's shocking, but it's meant to be. Nothing could more effectively belittle the devils.

[1] *Milton's P.L.* (1951), p. 17.
[2] p. 39.
[3] 'Milton' (1839), *Works* (1862–3), vi. 321, 322 n.
[4] p. 35.

Bentley seems to me to be helpful, too, when he objects to the leviathan 'slumbring on the Norway foam' (I. 203). 'We allow *Foam* to be sometimes put for Sea or *Water* by our best Poets. . . . But here it comes unhappily; for it must be very solid Foam, that can support a sleeping Whale.'[1] This to me brings out how unobtrusively important is the word *foam*. There *is* something sinister and mysterious, something of black magic, about Satan the leviathan. Once we notice the word *foam*, we see that the effect is very like that other moment of horror twenty lines later, when Satan is

> Aloft, incumbent on the dusky Air
> That felt unusual weight. (I. 226–7)

And it is not just the similarity of the idea that links the two passages together (and in so doing explains the poetic power of *foam*)—the phrases are linked too by their exactly parallel syntax. 'Slumbring on the Norway foam': 'Incumbent on the dusky Air.' Adjective . . . on the . . . adjective . . . noun (in each case, one of the elements). Perhaps even the echoing in *slumbring/incumbent* does something to tie the two phrases together. But in any case the parallelism of idea seems to me enough to yoke the phrases. In which case, it is not irresponsible to apply the words 'that felt unusual weight' not only to the air but also to the foam. Bentley in a way was right to remark that 'it must be very solid Foam, that can support a sleeping Whale'. But as is often the case with an anti-Miltonist, we can disagree with him and find the phrase moving and relevant in its sinister mystery.

There would be little point in trying to defend all the passages which the modern anti-Miltonists have attacked. When Mr. Eliot faintly praised the leviathan simile, he was endorsed by Dr. Leavis: 'Miltonic similes don't focus one's perception of the relevant, or sharpen definition in any way.'[2] Likewise with the *sit/stand* inconsistency. It would be foolish to claim that all the disputed passages are of this fairly straightforward kind, a kind where it can plausibly be sug-

[1] pp. 10–11. [2] *The Common Pursuit*, p. 22.

gested that there has been a misreading. But it is as well to remember that there are such things as simple misreadings.

The charges against Milton, then, can be simply classified. First, there are misreadings. Second, there are convincing accounts either of general faults in the Miltonic style, or of particular moments when the poet's mind was not fully on what he was doing. Third, there are the large-scale accusations of imprecision and insensitivity.

But before I try to defend the style against these last accusations, I must first concede that it cannot always be defended. There are moments when the language seems to be manipulated more from habit than from inner necessity. There are aridities, such as the digestion of the angels (v. 433–43). There is the 'untransmuted lump of futurity' at the end: 'and what makes it worse is that the actual writing in this passage is curiously bad' (C. S. Lewis).[1] Dr. Broadbent says trenchantly that ' "*Egypt*, divided by the River *Nile*" is one of the worst lines of verse in English and demeans every previous reference in the poem to Pharaoh, the Nile, the Red Sea, Moses'.[2]

But the occasions when the verse falters seem most often to be those that are also open to general complaint. 'He does even to a *Miracle* suit his *Speech* to his *Subject*'[3] (1694)—so when the subject is hollow, the speech is too. The verse (honourably, in a way) fails to keep up the pretence that all is well.

Let me take one passage to illustrate an important (though infrequent) failing of the style, its insensitive over-emphasis. Milton has recourse to such over-emphasis when he is trapped by some difficulty or other. For example, the narrative inconsistencies into which he is forced are nowhere clearer than in the War in Heaven. Voltaire in 1727 pro-

[1] *A Preface*, p. 125. In *E. & S.* (1958), F. T. Prince has shown that such futurity was both traditional and necessary; he has not shown that the section is well written. Addison complained of Book XII: 'in some Places the Author has been so attentive to his Divinity, that he has neglected his Poetry' (*The Spectator*, No. 369, 3 May 1712).

[2] *Some Graver Subject* (1960), pp. 279–80.

[3] 'To Mr. T. S. in Vindication of *P.L.*' (Spingarn, iii. 199).

tested at 'the visible Contradiction which reigns in that Episode', since God commands his troops to *drive them out*: 'How does it come to pass, after such a positive Order, that the Battle hangs doubtful? And why did God the Father command *Gabriel* and *Raphael*, to do what he executes afterwards by his Son only.'[1] And Mr. Peter[2] has skilfully and wittily analysed this muddle.

In God's speech to the Messiah, the painful hesitation that comes over the verse is made the clearer by the magnificent lines which begin and end the speech—lines which are not uneasy because they depend not upon the story but upon an intuition. But the speech itself is most disappointing:

> two dayes are past,
> Two dayes, as we compute the dayes of Heav'n,
> Since Michael and his Powers went forth to tame
> These disobedient; sore hath been thir fight,
> As likeliest was, when two such Foes met arm'd;
> For to themselves I left them, and thou knowst,
> Equal in their Creation they were form'd,
> Save what sin hath impaird, which yet hath wrought
> Insensibly, for I suspend thir doom;
> Whence in perpetual fight they needs must last
> Endless, and no solution will be found:
> Warr wearied hath perform'd what Warr can do,
> And to disorder'd rage let loose the reines,
> With Mountains as with Weapons arm'd, which makes
> Wild work in Heav'n, and dangerous to the maine.
> Two dayes are therefore past, the third is thine;
> For thee I have ordain'd it, and thus farr
> Have sufferd, that the Glorie may be thine
> Of ending this great Warr, since none but Thou
> Can end it . . . (VI. 684–703)

As Mr. Empson has said, 'The recent objections to the style of *Paradise Lost* seem to me wrong-headed when Milton is using it to say something real, but they do apply to the Sixth Book.'[3]

[1] *An Essay upon the Civil Wars of France, and also upon the Epic Poetry of the European Nations* (1727), pp. 119–20.

[2] *A Critique of P.L.* (1960), pp. 77–84.

[3] *Milton's God* (1961), pp. 54–55.

First, Milton mistakenly tries to make the argument run smoothly (a thing it could never do) by greasing it with asides. But all they do is emphasize the staginess by which one member of the Trinity speaks to another. 'Two dayes, *as we compute the dayes of Heav'n*': not only is this a flabby footnote, but it is one that is utterly inappropriate as spoken to the Messiah, who hardly needs to be told it. There is the same weakness in 'as likeliest was' (all too likely, might murmur Voltaire), or in 'and thou knowst'. Such phrases in another context might have helped to give the impression that the argument was unfolding in easy stages. But here they are made absurd by the Messiah's omniscience—it is pointless to say 'and thou knowst' to someone who is omniscient.[1] The phrase rings as falsely as the famous interchange from *The Critic*, which also fastens on the characteristic pedantry about the passing of time:

> *Sir Walter.* You know, my friend, scarce two revolving suns,
> And three revolving moons, have closed their course,
> Since haughty Philip, in despight of peace,
> With hostile hand hath struck at England's trade,
> *Sir Christopher.* ——I know it well.
> *Sir Walter.* Philip you know is proud Iberia's king!
> *Sir Christopher.* He is.
>
> (Act II, scene ii)

The whole of God's speech is betrayed by this narrative difficulty into a wordiness that is meant to disguise the muddle. 'Equal in their Creation they were form'd': this merely duplicates 'They were formed equal' and 'They were equal in their creation'. A 'perpetual fight' is sure to be 'endless'. The difference between 'perform' and 'do' is merely metrical when we hear that 'Warr wearied hath perform'd what Warr can do'. Similarly in such a context 'arm'd' already means 'with Weapons', so those words are hardly needed.

[1] Mr. Peter says of Book III: 'Two divinities cannot discuss what must be known to them both like this without at least one of them appearing fallible' (*A Critique*, p. 13).

And there are other weaknesses. There is the inept introduction of the effects of sin—immediately cancelled in an afterthought. There is the bathos of 'and no solution will be found', and the rather empty use of 'let loose the reines', which would in this context have come fully alive with the help of a word or two. And there is the dangerous ambiguity of *suffered*: 'and thus far have sufferd'.

As Bagehot saw, 'by a curiously fatal error, Milton has selected for delineation exactly that part of the Divine nature which is most beyond the reach of the human faculties, and which is also, when we try to describe our fancy of it, the least effective to our minds. He has made God *argue*.'[1]

It is at such moments that something goes wrong with Milton's style.

> But all conventions have their pomp
> And all styles can come down to noise.

Yet it is very seldom that the style of *Paradise Lost* comes down to noise, and (having made a few concessions) I shall now turn to the positive qualities of the Grand Style. But to conclude this introductory chapter, I must say something briefly about the question of 'reading things into' a poet.

Plainly there is no theory or dial which will tell whether or not a particular critical insight is true. We cannot expect *proof*; but we have a right to some degree of substantiation—an insight must be plausible. Naturally there are moments when critics may seem to be proclaiming 'the more the merrier'—the more suggestions, or ambiguities, or paradoxes, the better the poem. But one's objections may not be to their creed, but to the particular moments when their creed does not fit the evidence, when it demands that we reject the different kinds of substantiation to which one may appeal: the aptness of the insight itself, both locally and in the poem as a whole; the practice of the poet elsewhere; the practice of his contemporaries; the observations of his critics, especially the earliest ones; and so on. In each case there will

[1] 1859. *Literary Studies* (1905), ii. 212.

be a unique balance of evidence. My own *general* position is very like Mr. Empson's:

> If one view makes a bit of poetry very good, and another makes it very bad, the author's intention is inherently likely to be the one that makes it good; especially if we know that he writes well sometimes. . . . To try to make a printed page mean something good is only fair. There is a question for a critic at what point this generous and agreeable effort of mind ought to stop, and with an old text (the *Hamlet* of Shakespeare for example) it is no use to impute a meaning which the intended readers or audience could not have had in mind, either consciously or unconsciously.[1]

Yet, naturally enough, I do not agree with all Mr. Empson's particular insights; some of them—and each would have to be argued separately—seem to me improbable. He is, I think, in danger of giving a false primacy to the fact that the insight makes the poetry better. There is something risky in a formulation like 'Such a critic will often impute to an author a meaning too nasty-minded for the author to have intended . . . '.[2] After all, some authors are very nasty-minded. The beauty of an insight is certainly one piece of evidence about it—but no single such point can claim an absolute majority over the other kinds of substantiation. Though the following pages owe everything to Empsonian criticism, they try to slow down the process which in Mr. Empson is so agonizingly nimble. They try to offer, wherever possible, some kind of substantiation. That is why I have made so much use of Milton's earliest commentators. And if I too am sometimes anxious about the 'more the merrier' critics (and about my own leaning), the school seems to me preferable to the one whose dusty answer seems to be 'the *less* the merrier', and which takes a lugubrious relish in trying to scotch any close criticism which might suggest that a poet's use of words is subtle, delicate, ingenious, or new.

[1] *Milton's God*, p. 28.
[2] *Milton's God*, p. 230.

2. The Grand Style

ANY critic of Milton cowers away from discussing his Grand Style, since the great tributes to its power and sublimity have already been paid. Is there any need to add anything to Arnold? 'He is our great artist in style, our one first-rate master in the grand style.'[1] Or to Johnson? 'The characteristick quality of his poem is sublimity. He sometimes descends to the elegant, but his element is the great. He can occasionally invest himself with grace; but his natural port is gigantick loftiness. He can please when pleasure is required; but it is his peculiar power to astonish.'[2]

Certainly the traditions of grandeur within which *Paradise Lost* lives are obvious enough: the heroic example of Homer and Virgil, the sublimity of the Bible, the European dignity of a style that deliberately does not limit itself to the vernacular. And that Milton's is a Grand Style is granted even by those who dislike his verse. Their argument is not that it is not grand, but that its grandeur forfeits the possibility of delicacy and subtlety.

That his style astonishes is itself some cause for surprise. The epic is of all literary kind the most dignified, the most concerned to fulfil expectation rather than to baffle or ignore it. It is true that any work of literature must be both surprising and just, but the proportions of each will vary greatly. To be ridiculous is even more damaging to the epic poet than to be predictable. Yet he must combine two fervours: a heroic dedication to tradition; and a heroic dedication to

[1] 'A French Critic on Milton' (1877. *Mixed Essays*).

[2] *Lives of the Poets*, ed. Hill, i. 177.

himself, a confidence in his own greatness which will prevent his suffocating under the weight of a great tradition:

> Oft times nothing profits more
> Then self-esteem, grounded on just and right
> Well manag'd.

We hear often enough that Milton was a great egotist; but he was a great egotist who yet chose on all occasions to work within literary traditions of a strictness that has awed and stifled others. (The 'egotistical sublime' is, after all, something of a paradox—Hazlitt, too, saw that Wordsworth's Muse was 'distinguished by a proud humility'.) In his dedication to the past, Milton chooses the cruel and rewarding circumscriptions which provide an artistic analogy to the moral laws 'whose service is perfect freedom'. Self-abnegation and even 'some narrow place enclos'd' need not be enervating, as his last great hero insisted when he challenged Harapha.

This chapter on the Grand Style selects four important Miltonic topics: rhythm or music, syntax, metaphor, and word-play.[1] To examine what has been said about Milton's rhythms and music is soon to realize that here we have one of the elements of the Grand Style which is both indisputably important and almost impossible to analyse. That Milton's sound-effects are magnificent is not denied even by his detractors—how could they deny it, since their accusation is that he lavishes on his music the attention that ought to be spent on his sense?

There follow the three topics that seem to me fruitful as well as important, and with each of them I have tried to show how, in this Grand Style, certain effects were and others were not possible. The key to any understanding of the Grand Style is decorum: 'What the laws are of a true *Epic* Poem, what of a *Dramatic*, what of a *Lyric*, what Decorum is, which

[1] An obvious omission here is Milton's rhetoric. I have not dealt with it mainly because its technical nature would be at odds with the approach used elsewhere. Moreover, I could not emulate Dr. J. B. Broadbent, who deals with it in *Some Graver Subject*, and in 'Milton's Rhetoric' (*Modern Philology*, 1959)—an article which succeeds in using such a study to make genuinely critical points.

is the grand master-piece to observe' (Milton's *Of Education*). Decorum (in the sense both of epic tradition and of aptness to Milton's subject) demanded that he should elevate his style by deviating greatly from common usage. My account of his syntax tries first to establish just *how* Milton uses it to astonish, and then turns to the recent accusations against it. I have tried to refute them, and to establish that in deviating from normal usage Milton does not deviate from sense or sensitivity.

It is decorum, again, which explains Milton's use of metaphor. Here more has to be conceded to the anti-Miltonists; the Shakespearian metaphor did not suit Milton's traditions or his gifts. But this does not mean that he made no successful use of metaphorical effects in *Paradise Lost*—and it is possible to show what kind of metaphor was apt to the Grand Style, and how admirably Milton uses it. There is the same limitation and success in his word-play; once again both epic decorum and Milton's temperament virtually precluded certain bold effects of word-play, while encouraging unobtrusive felicities. I hope that it will be seen that, in my estimate of Milton's Grand Style, while much is taken very much more abides.

I. A NOTE ON RHYTHM AND MUSIC

It is clear that, as yet, effects of rhythm and music in verse have been found to offer little opportunity to the critic. Perhaps in Milton's case this need not be especially worrying, since usually even those who dislike his verse admit that it is not deficient here. True, Dr. Leavis complained about the monotony of the rhythm in *Paradise Lost*; but not many pages later he admitted that 'It is impossible to enforce a judgment about rhythm by written analysis and difficult to do so in any way'.[1] De Quincey gave a wise warning about not being too quick to condemn Milton's rhythms: 'You may be put down with shame by some man reading the line

[1] *Revaluation*, p. 64.

otherwise, reading it with a different emphasis, a different caesura, or perhaps a different suspension of the voice, so as to bring out a new and self-justifying effect.'[1]

The other danger in discussing rhythm and music is that it is more entangled with the merely subjective than any other kind of criticism. A notorious example is Dr. Leavis's remark about Keats's *moss'd cottage-trees*: 'It is not fanciful, I think, to find that (the sense being what it is) the pronouncing of "cottage-trees" suggests, too, the crisp bite and the flow of juice as the teeth close in the ripe apple.'[2] But if this is not fanciful, then what is? It is absurd to try to support the fantasy with 'the sense being what it is'—as if these words were about apples. They are not, they are about 'moss'd cottage-trees', and if we want to insist on the sense, we will have to say that the words sound like teeth meeting not in a ripe apple but in moss and wood. As Dr. Johnson said, 'it is scarcely to be doubted, that on many occasions we make the musick which we imagine ourselves to hear, that we modulate the poem by our own disposition, and ascribe to the numbers the effects of the sense'.[3]

The point is not that such criticism is self-evidently untrue—it is that it self-evidently has very little to do with 'known Causes and rational Deduction' (Johnson's area of criticism). This is clear from Mr. James Whaler and Mr. Arnold Stein, both of whom provide on other Miltonic subjects much useful and rational criticism. Mr. Whaler has analysed the rhythm of the line describing Satan as a wolf who 'Leaps o're the fence with ease into the Fould' (IV. 187): 'The initial spondee is the crouch before the spring. The constricted front vowel in "leaps" is the muscular tension at the moment of leaping. The open back-vowel in "o'er" eases that tension as the brute body attains mid-flight in its vault. The undulatory vowel-sequence, "fence"—"ease", "-to"—"fold", reinforced by nodal pauses before and after "with ease", echoes the agile arc traced by the intruder. The

[1] 'Milton *versus* Southey and Landor' (1847). *Works* (1862–3), xi. 189.

[2] *The Common Pursuit*, p. 16.

[3] *The Rambler*, No. 94 (9 Feb. 1751).

uncertain inversion of the light-stressed foot, "into", lands the wolf quivering with success at reaching his goal.'[1]

All the ringing phrases seem to me pure imagination—the brute body, quivering with success, the agile arc, and so on. And how can it be true that 'the initial spondee is the crouch before the spring' when the meaning of the words insists that the wolf *leaps* with the very first syllable?

It is the same with Mr. Stein's comments on

> Then Both from out Hell Gates into the *w*aste
> *W*ide Anarchie of Chaos *d*amp and *d*ark
> Fle*w* *d*ivers. (x. 282–4)

'The rhythmic impulse of the *w–w* is upward and outward, of the *d–d* downward. The final *w–d*, if it represents anything, is certainly different; the *w* is less upward and the *d* less downward; if they have not reversed their directions they have at least compromised them, perhaps under the influence of chaos.'[2]

The influence of chaos has perhaps reached farther than Mr. Stein envisaged—his argument seems to me impressive in its confidence but worthless in its inaccessibility to the ordinary processes of the mind. I should like to hear Mr. Stein say 'Fle*w*' so that it has a *w* in it.

If critics as intelligent as these can sink, it may be best to conclude that the close analysis of Milton's rhythms and music is

> A gulf profound as that Serbonian Bog
> Betwixt Damiata and mount Casius old,
> Where Armies whole have sunk.

A detour may be wiser. And as far as rhythm and music go, Milton's lines demand Hazlitt's fervour: 'The way to defend Milton against all impugners, is to take down the book and read it.'[3]

[1] *Counterpoint and Symbol* (*Anglistica VI*, 1956), p. 18.
[2] *Answerable Style* (1953), p. 149.
[3] *Lectures on the English Poets. Works* (ed. P. P. Howe, 1930), v. 61.

One of Dr. Johnson's most famous criticisms of Milton was prophetic of much of the twentieth-century dissatisfaction:

> The truth is, that both in prose and verse, he had formed his style by a perverse and pedantick principle. He was desirous to use English words with a foreign idiom. This in all his prose is discovered and condemned, for there judgement operates freely, neither softened by the beauty nor awed by the dignity of his thoughts; but such is the power of his poetry that his call is obeyed without resistance, the reader feels himself in captivity to a higher and a nobler mind, and criticism sinks in admiration. . . . Of him, at last, may be said what Jonson says of Spenser, that 'he wrote no language', but has formed what Butler calls 'a Babylonish Dialect', in itself harsh and barbarous, but made by exalted genius and extensive learning the vehicle of so much instruction and so much pleasure that, like other lovers, we find grace in its deformity.[1]

This is not quite to say, with the sturdy frankness of Dr. Leavis, 'we dislike his verse'. But it is clear that, for Johnson, Milton's verse was good in spite of his deviation from normal English, not because of it. The reader willingly puts up with the deformity, but there is no doubt about its being a deformity.

Plainly there are times when Milton deviates from the usual word-order for the bad reason that he is in the habit of it. And there are times when he does so for the inadequate and well-known reason that the result sounds more magniloquent, or—in Addison's phrase—'to give his Verse the greater Sound, and throw it out of Prose'. Yet it is interesting that Addison went on to say, 'I must confess, that I think his Stile, tho' admirable in general, is in some Places too much stiffened and obscured by the frequent Use of those Methods, which *Aristotle* has prescribed for the raising of it'.[2] But this, as he saw, does not apply to the usual run of the verse, in which the syntax is meaningfully controlled with great success.

[1] *Lives of the Poets*, ed. Hill, i. 190–1.
[2] *The Spectator*, No. 285 (26 Jan. 1712).

Its first success is obvious enough: his natural port was gigantic loftiness. Milton achieves this loftiness as much by word-order as by the sonority, dignity or weight of the words themselves. Mr. Eliot has put the positive side excellently:

> It is only in the period that the wave-length of Milton's verse is to be found: it is his ability to give a perfect and unique pattern to every paragraph, such that the full beauty of the line is found in its context, and his ability to work in larger musical units than any other poet—that is to me the most conclusive evidence of Milton's supreme mastery. The peculiar feeling, almost a physical sensation of a breathless leap, communicated by Milton's long periods, and by his alone, is impossible to procure from rhymed verse.[1]

The power and sublimity of a 'breathless leap' are there in the opening lines of the poem:

> Of Mans First Disobedience, and the Fruit
> Of that Forbidden Tree, whose mortal tast
> Brought Death into the World, and all our woe,
> With loss of Eden, till one greater Man
> Restore us, and regain the blissful Seat,
> Sing Heav'nly Muse . . .

Matthew Arnold[2] acutely commented: 'So chary of a sentence is he, so resolute not to let it escape him till he has crowded into it all he can, that it is not till the thirty-ninth word in the sentence that he will give us the key to it, the word of action, the verb.'

But such withholding of the verb 'sing' (*Of Mans First Disobedience . . . Sing*) might be no more than perverse. Its justification is in the heroic way that it states the magnitude of the poem's subject and so the magnitude of its task

(*Disobedience . . . Death . . . woe . . . loss of Eden . . . one greater Man*),

while still insisting that this vastness is within the poet's compass. The word-order quite literally encompasses the huge themes. 'Where couldst thou words of such a compass

[1] 'Milton II.' *On Poetry and Poets*, pp. 157–8.

[2] *On Translating Homer*, III (1861).

find?' asked Marvell, wondering at Milton's achievement of his *vast Design*: 'a Work so infinite he spann'd'.

A poet is always insisting, as if by magic, that his control of words is a control of experience; and here we are given a 'breathless' sense of Milton's *adventrous Song* with at the same time a reassuring sense of how firmly it is within his control. The curve of the sentence is not discursive—however wide the gyre, this falcon hears its falconer.

The verb is, as Arnold saw, the 'key' to the sentence—in the sense that it embodies Milton's power to open the subjects of his poem. Yet we would not be very interested in, or impressed by, a key unless we had first been given some idea of what riches we will be shown.

'So *resolute* not to let it escape him . . .', said Arnold, and the word may be used as a transition to a fine comment by Mr. Empson. He quotes Valdes's lines to Faustus, lines which deliberately hold back until the end the ominous condition *If learned Faustus will be resolute*:

> Faustus,
> These books, thy wit, and our experience,
> Shall make all nations to canonise us.
> As Indian moors obey their Spanish lords
> So shall the spirits of every element
> Be always serviceable to us three;
> Like lions shall they guard us when we please,
> Like Almain rutters, with their horsemen's staves,
> Or Lapland giants, trotting by our sides,
> Sometimes like women, or unwedded maids
> Shadowing more beauty in their airy brows
> Than have the white breasts of the queen of love:
> From Venice shall they drag huge argosies,
> And from America the golden fleece
> That yearly stuffs old Philip's treasury;
> If learned Faustus will be resolute.

'That a conditional clause should have been held back through all these successive lightnings of poetry, that after their achievement it should still be present with the same conviction and *resolution*, is itself a statement of heroic character.'[1] That is nobly said, and such heroism is one of Milton's glories too. He is even able to sustain such effects over vaster distances. Though his single lines may not be mightier than Marlowe's, his sentences often are.

Take Belial's reply to Moloch during the council in Hell. Moloch has asked rhetorically 'what can be worse than to dwell here,' and Belial seizes the phrase and holds it aloft:

> What can we suffer worse? is this then worst,
> Thus sitting, thus consulting, thus in Arms?

And at once he launches his argument, wheeling through six lines with a hawk's-eye view of their past torments, and plunging home with *that sure was worse*. But that telling reminder offers no pause, and Belial circles again, this time above their future torments. He drives relentlessly through 'what if . . . or . . . what if . . .', and then sweeps to his annihilating climax, foreseen and deliberately held back:

> What if the breath that kindl'd those grim fires
> Awak'd should blow them into sevenfold rage
> And plunge us in the Flames? or from above
> Should intermitted vengeance Arme again
> His red right hand to plague us? what if all
> Her stores were op'n'd, and this Firmament
> Of Hell should spout her Cataracts of Fire,
> Impendent horrors, threatning hideous fall
> One day upon our heads; while we perhaps
> Designing or exhorting glorious Warr,
> Caught in a fierie Tempest shall be hurl'd
> Each on his rock transfixt, the sport and prey
> Of racking whirlwinds, or for ever sunk
> Under yon boyling Ocean, wrapt in Chains;
> There to converse with everlasting groans,
> Unrespited, unpitied, unrepreevd,
> Ages of hopeless end; this would be worse. (II. 170–86)

When a sentence surges forward like that, the end of it seems less a destination than a destiny.

[1] *Seven Types of Ambiguity* (1930; 2nd ed., 1947), p. 32.

It is this ability to harness the thrust of his syntax which sustains Milton's great argument—even the smallest passages have a dynamic force of the astonishing kind which one finds almost everywhere in Dickens. And lines which one has long admired for their brilliant succinctness, lines like 'Better to reign in Hell, then serve in Heav'n' which from one point of view have the free-standing strength of proverbs —even such lines take on greater force when they come as the clinching of a surge of feeling:

> What matter where, if I be still the same,
> And what I should be, all but less then hee
> Whom Thunder hath made greater? Here at least
> We shall be free; th' Almighty hath not built
> Here for his envy, will not drive us hence:
> Here we may reign secure, and in my choyce
> To reign is worth ambition though in Hell:
> Better to reign in Hell, then serve in Heav'n. (I. 256–63)

It is easy to see how much the power of the last line is created by its context if we remember Dryden's setting in *The State of Innocence*. In Dryden the line is witty:

> Chang'd as we are, we'er yet from Homage free;
> We have, by Hell, at least, gain'd liberty:
> That's worth our fall; thus low tho' we are driven,
> Better to Rule in Hell, than serve in Heaven. (Act I)

Yet in Milton the line was not the less witty for being heroic.

III. SYNTAX AND SENSE

For Milton, the stars in their dance were

> Eccentric, intervolv'd, yet regular
> Then most, when most irregular they seem. (V. 623–4)

For many of Milton's critics, his words are merely eccentric, intervolved and irregular. But just as it was useful to start by looking at the Milton controversy, so it is as well to study the specific criticisms of Milton's word-order that have been made by those who agree with Dr. Leavis. Do Milton's syntactical effects make his style not grand but grandiose? Mr. John Peter's examples must be considered, leading as they naturally do to a discussion of tortuousness in the Grand Style, and from there to Dr. Davie's important and—I hope—mistaken analysis of Milton's syntax. Hostile criticism often deserves the compliment of rational opposition—there is something Philistine about Mr. Douglas Bush's manly view that 'As for his syntax, it never troubles those who leave it alone'.[1] So now we know—but do we? It would not really do, at any rate, to treat Mr. Peter and Dr. Davie as if they were meddling children who won't leave well alone.

Mr. Peter's *Critique of Paradise Lost* is much less telling in its criticism of the style than of the events in the poem. In fact he seems to me altogether more successful when he points out Milton's stylistic successes. He has, for example, an excellent discussion of the many oxymorons in the early books, and the way in which larger passages have 'the same kind of vitality, on a diffuse scale, that an oxymoron has succinctly'.[2] That is, a vibrancy which makes us struggle to reconcile two views of the fallen angels, and which 'finally leaves the verse with a special forcefulness, imparting to the devils themselves a striking and enigmatic fascination'.

But when Mr. Peter gives a page of examples of Milton's bad syntax, he unfortunately omits to say just what is wrong, merely introducing them with: 'This readiness to assume that certain ideas have been fully absorbed and integrated into the poem when they have not is roughly analogous to a common fault in the epic's style, a fault which is all too easy to exemplify.'[3] That kind of brisk evasion Mr. Peter learned from Dr. Leavis, who often practises a large economy to save analysis: 'But a comparison will save analysis. . . .'

[1] *English Literature in the Earlier 17th Century* (1945), p. 389.

[2] p. 39. In *The French Biblical Epic in the 17th Century* (1955, pp. 159, 218) Dr. R. A. Sayce shows how Saint-Amant and Coras use oxymoron (e.g. *douce imposture*) to disguise moral uncertainties. Milton's use of what Dr. Sayce calls 'a figure which in its condensed violence is perhaps especially characteristic of baroque poetry' is the more valid one that Mr. Peter sums up as 'enigmatic fascination'.

[3] p. 161.

Yet it is impossible to say that there is something wrong with the syntax of a few lines from Milton unless one first considers the context. And Milton deserves the compliment of clear rather than muttered complaint.

Nor can one even catch what complaint is being muttered when Mr. Peter offers as his first example that admirable line describing Satan's destination as 'His journies end and our beginning woe' (III. 633). What is wrong with it? It seems perfectly straightforward, memorable and succinct, so simple and clear as to withstand any charge of being un-English. The 'un-English' of *Scrutiny* critics is always in danger of turning into the vague and apoplectic splutter which goes with *unBritish*.

Mr. Peter's next example is a better one for his argument, Satan's angry jibe at Michael during the war:

> Hast thou turnd the least of these
> To flight, or if to fall, but that they rise
> Unvanquisht, easier to transact with mee
> That thou shouldst hope, imperious, & with threats
> To chase me hence? (VI. 284–8)

The opening and closing phrases strike with strong clarity; and the belated 'imperious' breaks out with an angry scorn that is dramatically apt. But it would be hard to defend the inversion in 'easier to transact with me that thou shouldst hope'. True, it thrusts the contempt of *easier* on us straightaway, but this is perhaps not enough recompense for what seems inappropriately circuitous, pedantry rather than oratory. The lines are not at all obscure, and so ought not to incur disproportionate censure; but they hardly show Miltonic inversion at its expressive best.

It is un-English tortuousness which Mr. Peter presumably dislikes in his next example, the lines describing the life on the Earth after the Creation:

> Aire, Water, Earth,
> By Fowl, Fish, Beast, was flown, was swum, was walkt
> Frequent. (VII. 502–4)

But are the lines bad? (One would first have to remember that 'frequent' here means 'crowded, full'.) The lines certainly are artificial and complicated, but why shouldn't they be? They are not wilfully so, but because Milton needs to suggest both the teeming activity of the Earth, and the fundamental order and harmony of it. So he presents an active throng of monosyllables while at the same time grouping them into a pattern of triplets. Landor elsewhere disliked such a use of passive verbs: 'This Latinism is inadmissible; there is no loophole in our language for its reception.'[1] But the point of the passive verbs is to insist, as Hopkins might, that at last the great elements of the Earth which God had earlier created are being used according to his plan. The Earth is there to be walked, and the water to be swum. The immediately preceding words bring this out:

> Earth in her rich attire
> Consummate lovly smil'd.

That is, rejoices and is beautiful in being consummated, completed and made use of. All that is still wanted is man,

> the Master work, the end
> Of all yet don.

Not that these lines show Milton at his best. But they do give a sense of the thronging life of the Earth which is yet, unlike that presented by Comus, ordered into the divine harmony of 'trinal triplicities'. Nor are the passive verbs merely clumsy. They are to bring out what the air, water, and earth are for—the purposeful magnanimity of the Creation. It is because the air was flown that God most deeply saw that it was good.

Still with disapproval, but still without comment, Mr. Peter then quotes the closing words of a speech when Eve argues with Adam about leaving him:

> Thoughts, which how found they harbour in thy brest,
> Adam, missthought of her to thee so dear? (IX. 288–9)

[1] *Imaginary Conversations*: 'Southey and Landor'. *Works*, ed. T. E. Welby (1927–31), v. 259.

The lines are admittedly tortuous, and they may well use a foreign idiom. But perhaps they *use* it, rather than merely copy it. Is tortuousness out of keeping here? Eve is hurt by Adam's 'unkindness', and she is also keen to get her own way. She starts naturally enough with 'Thoughts, which . . .', and then breaks across with the indignation of a more direct syntax, a hurt question: 'how found they harbour in thy brest?' And then, with a fine austereness, she condemns the thoughts as *missthought*, and ends with the time-honoured appeal, 'how could you think such things of me?'—'miss-thought of her to thee so dear'. The word-order unfolds with admirable psychological truth, and it combines in exactly the right proportions the pathos, the indignation, and the tearfulness.[1] That such is the intention is plain from the line that follows: 'To whom with healing words Adam reply'd.'

If there is anything wrong with the syntax, it is the opposite of what would be suggested by Mr. Peter's disapproval: not that the word-order is meaninglessly contorted, but that it makes too thorough-going an effort to trace the contours of thought becoming speech—the sort of well-intentioned extremism which one finds in Hopkins or Joyce at their less successful.

The final example which Mr. Peter offers for our condemnation comes from the Son's intercession for Man to the Father:

> Let him live
> Before thee reconcil'd, at least his days
> Numberd, though sad. (XI. 38–40)

Certainly this is characteristically Miltonic—it exactly fits Mr. Empson's unforgettable account of 'the sliding, sideways, broadening movement, normal to Milton'.[2] But the lines are to me characteristically good rather than bad. They beautifully combine two kinds of movement, forward and spinning, like that triumphant line 'Erroneous, there to

[1] Richardson said: 'the Note of Interrogation at the end of the Sentence gives a Poignancy to it' (p. 405)—*poignancy* in 1734 meaning more 'piercing' than 'pathetic'.

[2] *Some Versions*, p. 162.

wander and forlorne'. Raleigh reminded us that 'De Quincey speaks of the "slow planetary wheelings" of Milton's verse, and the metaphor is a happy one; the verse revolves on its axis at every line, but it always has another motion, and is related to a more distant centre'.[1]

It may seem strange that Matthew Arnold should have spoken of the 'self-retarding movement' of Milton's verse, for what verse has greater momentum? Yet Arnold was right. Though one of the movements drives forward, the other is circling on itself. The Grand Style has the energy of Satan, who 'Throws his steep flight in many an Aerie wheele'. Or the energy of the stars, with 'their various motions'. In serene lines like those of the interceding Son, the style even has the various motions of the Earth itself:

> Or Shee from West her silent course advance
> With inoffensive pace that spinning sleeps
> On her soft Axle, while she paces Eev'n,
> And bears thee soft with the smooth Air along. (VIII. 163–6)

The Leavisite position assumes that Milton's style is continuously grand, and therefore continuously deviating from the usual spoken or written word-order. This is an odd idea to have about a poet who begins the most important book of his epic with the laconic audacity of

> No more of talk where God or Angel Guest . . .

That must be the least pompous opening anywhere in a sublime poem, and it is to that quiet brittleness that we owe the full power of the lines that follow, the lines that on an age-old anvil wince and sing:

> Anger and just rebuke, and judgement giv'n,
> That brought into this World a world of woe . . .

And many of the memorable lines in Milton have the directness of 'No more of talk . . .'. Satan asking 'What matter where, if I be still the same'. Belial broken in one descriptive

[1] *Milton* (1900), p. 192. F. T. Prince has an interesting account of the sources of this syntactical pattern (*The Italian Element in Milton's Verse*, 1954, pp. 112–19).

phrase, 'A fairer person lost not Heav'n'. Eve in love with Adam:

> from his Lip
> Not Words alone pleas'd her—

admirable in that it means exactly what it says, and is neither a high-minded 'Puritan' sneer at the Lip, nor a low-minded cynical sneer at the Words:

> O when meet now
> Such pairs, in Love and mutual Honour joyn'd?

Or Adam presumptuously thinking that God will look silly if now that they have fallen he destroys them:

> least the Adversary
> Triumph and say; Fickle their State whom God
> Most Favors, who can please him long? Mee first
> He ruind, now Mankind; whom will he next? (IX. 947–50)

The important thing about the syntax there is the way that the brusque simplicity of 'who can please him long?' and 'whom will he next?' is played against the grand inversions of 'Fickle their State . . .' and 'Mee first he ruind'. The laconic and the colloquial burst out all the more strongly.

Mr. Hallett Smith has pointed to this in Adam's words after his creation, where 'the Latinized elliptical construction' of the second line 'suddenly resolves itself with ease and grace' in the next:

> Tell me, how may I know him, how adore,
> From whom I have that thus I move and live,
> And feel that I am happier then I know. (VIII. 280–2)

One might add that the unusual complication of the second line is in contrast with simplicity, not only externally, but also internally. Internally, in that the words themselves (as distinct from their order) are very uncomplicated and usual —they stand for the most basic of ideas. Externally, in that the complicated construction is immediately succeeded by straightforward simplicity. 'There could hardly be more natural and inevitable English than this', says Mr. Hallett

Smith.[1] And it is the natural last line that is the *raison d'être* of the sentence. The second line departs from English not because Milton has a 'callousness to the intrinsic nature of English' (Dr. Leavis), but because he values that intrinsic nature and wishes us to feel its power. It is not easy for a poet to put power behind such simplicity, especially in a poem the subject and genre of which forbid too colloquial a style. Mr. John Crowe Ransom has said that 'we should be so much in favor of tragedy and irony as not to think it good policy to require them in all our poems, for fear we might bring them into bad fame'.[2] In the same spirit, we might say that we should be so in favour of natural English as not to require it in all our poems, or throughout all our poems. At any rate, this seems less implausible than the view that the author of the closing lines of *Paradise Lost* was callous to the English language.

Often we find that the complication not only prepares the way for an energetic simplicity, but is also dramatically apt. The lines describing Satan's search for Eve build up through a pattern of repetitions that dramatically enacts Satan's repeated seeking and restless wishing, until Eve is spied—and at that point we break into a clearing, a line of verse which has neither the link of repetition which is in all the preceding lines, nor the endless spilling run-over into the next line: instead a simple single Marlovian line.

> He sought them both, but wish'd his hap might find
> Eve separate, he wish'd, but not with hope
> Of what so seldom chanc'd, when to his wish,
> Beyond his hope, Eve separate he spies,
> Veil'd in a Cloud of Fragrance, where she stood . . . (IX. 421–5)[3]

In this patterning, sounds are as effective as meanings, so that *hap . . . hope . . . hope* weaves the same net as *wish'd . . . wish'd . . . wish*. That net is woven by Satan: Eve appears in the direct innocence of a veil.

[1] 'No Middle Flight', *Huntington Library Quarterly* (1951–2), xv. 162.

[2] Quoted by Arnold Stein for a different purpose, *E.L.H.* (1949), xvi. 133.

[3] R. M. Adams oddly calls the pattern here 'a kind of verbal frippery' (*Ikon*, 1955, p. 89).

Sometimes Milton uses this device almost to the point of self-parody, as when Satan meets Death. Milton's difficulty here is real enough. He has no wish at all to depart from the traditional representation of Death. He needs, in fact, to say what he does say: 'black it stood as night, fierce as ten furies, terrible as hell'. But how can he possibly put any grandeur into such conventional words? His method, which is here admittedly more expressive than subtle, is to work up to this traditional simplicity through an entanglement of philosophical doubts and difficulties—all until the point when we will realize the trenchancy of those traditional representations which can cut through the mesh:

> The other shape,
> If shape it might be call'd that shape had none
> Distinguishable in member, joynt, or limb,
> Or substance might be call'd that shadow seem'd,
> For each seem'd either; black it stood as Night,
> Fierce as ten Furies, terrible as Hell . . . (II. 666–71)

The power of this sort of syntax can be seen by comparing two similes in *Henry VI Part III*, where Richard is soliloquizing about his villainy. The first simile is straightforward; it proceeds through point by point correspondence, and has the clarity of an epic simile rather than the vigour of a dramatic one:

> Why then I do but dream on sovereignty,
> Like one that stands upon a promontory,
> And spies a far-off shore, where he would tread,
> Wishing his foot were equal with his eye,
> And chides the sea, that sunders him from thence,
> Saying, he'll lade it dry, to have his way;
> So do I wish the crown, being so far off . . .

But this same soliloquy includes a very different simile. As Richard tells how he is lost in a thorny wood, the clustering repetitions thicken around him until the climax cuts through them:

> And I, like one lost in a thorny wood,

That rents the thorns, and is rent with the thorns,
Seeking a way, and straying from the way,
Not knowing how to find the open air,
But toiling desperately to find it out,
Torment myself, to catch the English crown:
And from that torment I will free myself,
Or hew my way out with a bloody axe. (Act III, scene ii)

The last line cuts through the thorns as if it were itself an axe—and 'bloody axe' reminds us savagely what the thorns really are. It is not necessary, because of this simile, to say that the other one is poor—but its success is a smaller achievement. Yet in spite of what Dr. Leavis says, Milton's syntax seems to me to be at least as often like the dramatic simile as it is like the epic one.

For Donald Davie, 'Dr. Leavis's account of this Miltonic music (there are other musics, in other poems) seems more clearly just on each new reading.'[1] Certainly one of the surprising things about Dr. Davie's excellent book *Articulate Energy* was that 'An Inquiry into the Syntax of English Poetry' should wish to say so very little about Milton. But in the course of the book it turned out that Dr. Davie doesn't really think of Milton as *English* poetry. 'In order to get syntactical closeness, Landor treats the English language as if it were Latin. And even if we make Milton himself a special case, it must be admitted as a rule that "strength" is not worth this sort of sacrifice.'[2]

Then in his later study (in *The Living Milton*) Dr. Davie lucidly deplored most of the syntax in *Paradise Lost*. The essay seems to me more successful on successes than on failures, but it certainly provides a useful critical foothold. Not only is it a very interesting piece of criticism in its own right, but it is also devoted to a subject where there is all too little useful criticism.[3]

[1] 'Syntax and Music in *P.L.*', *The Living Milton*, p. 83.

[2] *Articulate Energy* (1955), p. 62.

[3] J. B. Broadbent has some excellent local comments on syntax (*Some Graver*

Dr. Davie begins by discussing two syntactical successes. First,

> Him the Almighty Power
> Hurld headlong flaming from th' Ethereal Skie
> With hideous ruine and combustion down
> To bottomless perdition, there to dwell
> In Adamantine Chains and penal Fire,
> Who durst defie th' Omnipotent to Arms. (I. 44–49)

The success here Dr. Davie described as *muscular*: 'The placing of "Him", "down" and "To", in particular, gives us the illusion as we read that our own muscles are tightening in panic as we experience in our own bodies a movement just as headlong and precipitate as the one described.' The second example presents Satan journeying through the mud of Chaos (II. 939–50): 'Milton crowds stressed syllables together so as to make the vocal exertion in reading image the physical exertion described. It is the reader, too, who flounders, stumbles, pushes doggedly on.'

Dr. Davie then turns from such 'muscular' or 'dramatic' effects to another kind of success where metre is played against syntax and word-order: *narrative* effects. By this, he means that 'the language is deployed, just as the episodes are in a story, so as always to provoke the question "And then?"—to provoke this question and to answer it in unexpected ways. If any arrangement of language is a sequence of verbal events, here syntax is employed so as to make the most of each word's eventfulness, so as to make each key-word, like each new episode in a well told story, at once surprising and just.' He quotes the invocation to Book III, pointing particularly to two effects. First,

> Then feed on thoughts, that voluntarie move
> Harmonious numbers . . .

'At the line-ending "move" seems intransitive, and as such wholly satisfying; until the swing on to the next line,

Subject, e.g. pp. 164, 184). So have the eighteenth-century editors (e.g. Richardson on 'If thou beest he . . .').

"Harmonious numbers", reveals it (a little surprise, but a wholly fair one) as transitive. This flicker of hesitation about whether the thoughts move only themselves, or something else, makes us see that the numbers aren't really "something else" but are the very thoughts themselves, seen under a new aspect; the placing of "move", which produces the momentary uncertainty about its grammar, ties together "thoughts" and "numbers" in a relation far closer than cause and effect'.

That is a very useful insight into Milton's style. And there follows a similarly acute and subtle commentary on the slight surprise in the word *Day*:

> Thus with the Year
> Seasons return, but not to me returns
> Day . . .

—where we would expect 'Spring'.

At which Dr. Davie makes his general point, that all such effects depend on the narrative question 'What happens next?', on the poet's realizing that language, unlike the pictorial arts, operates through time, 'in terms of successive events, each new sentence a new small action with its own sometimes complicated plot'. And this perception, as he rightly insists, is one 'which much of the most influential modern criticism—working as it does through spatial metaphors, talking of "the figure in the carpet", of tensions balanced and cancelling out inside structures—seems expressly designed to obscure'.

But at this point Dr. Davie enters the second section of his essay, and we meet the surprising statement that 'these effects are rather the exception than the rule. Neither kinetic and dramatic effect, as in the lines on Satan's fall, nor narrative and musical effect, as in the invocation to Light, are in evidence at all frequently as we read *Paradise Lost.*'

Surprising, in the first place, because the tone implies—and the later stages of the argument insist—that such effects ought to be the rule rather than the exception. Yet surely it is probable that most of the syntax used by any poet will be neither dramatic nor narrative, but simply expository and descriptive. Such effects are certainly an added beauty, as powerful in their way as metaphor. But no one demands that poetry should be all metaphor. Even if, as is so often done, we take Donne as the antithesis of Milton, such effects are still the exception rather than the rule. Dr. Davie is setting a mistaken standard here: he is asking for an all-pervasive syntactical density and activity that would be likely to produce too rich a style—an equivalent of *Finnegans Wake*, perhaps. And indeed Dr. Davie himself has elsewhere given a more realistic point of view: 'We may wonder whether the syntax of poetry can ever be aesthetically neutral, a matter of indifference. It can, however. It can be unremarkable, like a human frame that is neither close-knit nor loose-limbed, neither well- nor ill-proportioned, but just normal. Much syntax in poetry is of this kind, and is therefore not poetic syntax as I understand it'.[1]

Yet it would be a pity if there were very little 'poetic syntax' in Milton. At which, one comes to the second surprising point about the essay; that the examples are not so self-evidently bad as Dr. Davie assumes.

> Others with vast Typhoean rage more fell
> Rend up both Rocks and Hills, and ride the Air
> In whirlwind; Hell scarce holds the wilde uproar.
> As when Alcides from Oechalia Crown'd
> With conquest, felt th' envenom'd robe, and tore
> Through pain up by the roots Thessalian Pines,
> And Lichas from the top of Oeta threw
> Into th' Euboic Sea. (II. 539–46)

Dr. Davie says that 'where the line is not end-stopped, the swing of the reading eye or voice around the line-ending is not turned to poetically expressive use'. But then he at once has to make an exception of the first two lines, 'where we swing around the line-ending to come hard upon the energetic verb, "Rend" '. He then objects that 'there is no expressive or dramatic reason why "Air" should be separated in this way from "In whirlwind"—a phrase which merely

[1] *Articulate Energy*, p. 67.

dangles limply into the next line'. Yet this is surely to miss the utter difference in tone between the two phrases, 'Ride the Air' and 'In whirlwind'—a difference which is successfully emphasized by the line-break. 'Ride the Air' gives a momentary suggestion of serenity, of strong and calm control. 'In whirlwind' shatters this into 'wild uproar'.

'So with thy whirlwind them pursue', Milton had written in his translation of Psalm lxxxiii. And in *Paradise Lost* whirlwinds are always one of the torments that pursue the fallen angels, who are 'orewhelm'd with Floods and Whirlwinds', 'the sport and prey of racking whirlwinds'—who are condemned to a land 'beat with perpetual storms of Whirlwind', and who are defeated by Christ's chariot which 'forth rush'd with whirl-wind sound'.[1]

The fallen angels have no control, no calm, and their strength is that of rage and pain. Elsewhere the divine calm, the divine control and strength, demand the serenity of 'Crystallin' rather than the uproar of 'whirlwind':

> Hee on the wings of Cherub rode sublime
> On the Crystallin Skie . . . (VI. 771–2)

The fact is that Milton often uses half-lines like 'In whirlwind' to jar against the previous line, as in the final phrase of

> and with ambitious aim
> Against the Throne and Monarchy of God
> Rais'd impious War in Heav'n and Battel proud
> With vain attempt. (I. 41–44)

That deflates. Dr. Davie might say it 'dangles limply', but the limpness is that of Satan. Dr. Broadbent commented crisply on these lines: 'The very heavy final stress on "proud" lengthens the pause before the next line, so that "With vain attempt" comes as a surprising snort of derision.'[2]

Dr. Davie's next point is even more arguable. He quotes

[1] I. 77; II. 182, 589; VI. 749. For the whirlwind of God see Ezek. i. 4; Isa. lxvi. 15; Jer. xxx. 23; Amos i. 14. It is relevant that the name *Typhon* means *whirlwind*, as M. Y. Hughes notes in his ed. (1957).

[2] 'Milton's Hell', *E.L.H.* (1954), xxi. 163.

> Tore
> Through pain up by the roots Thessalian Pines,

and says that 'the interposition of "Through pain" precludes both of two possible dramatic effects—either the violence of "Tore" at the beginning of the line, or the even more effective muscularity of having "tore" separated by the line-ending from "Up" '.

But surely the line as written has an 'even more effective muscularity', in separating *tore* and *up* even more violently. The agonized word-order presents the knotted effort of Hercules. The writhing of the strength and of the pain are almost those of Laocoön. In fact the line seems an outstanding example for the first, not the second, section of Dr. Davie's essay.

On the last two lines,

> And Lichas from the top of Oeta threw
> Into th' Euboic Sea,

he remarks: 'The Latinate inversion of word-order means that as we launch out from "threw" into the last line, we are asking not "*What* was thrown?" but only the much less interesting question "thrown where?" In fact, this question is so unexciting that we don't even ask it; so that "Into th' Euboic Sea" hangs superfluous—the sentence could just as well have ended where the line ends, after "threw".'

Again this seems wrong-headed. It is not self-evident that 'What was thrown?' is a more interesting question than 'thrown where?' The impressive thing is not that Hercules was able to throw a man—that is not a superhuman feat of strength—but that he was able to throw him such a long way. No doubt there are contexts in which 'What was thrown?' is a much more interesting question, but it is odd to suppose that there is a Platonic quality of 'Interest' to which that question is always much closer. In this case, it seems clear that 'thrown where?' is more interesting, and that the sentence could not 'just have well have ended where the line ends'.

All of Dr. Davie's objections to this passage are interesting, and they raise important points about Milton's Grand Style—but all are very vulnerable. Indeed, considering his charges, as so often in Milton criticism, brings out just how good the lines are. The same is true of another example:

> Th' undaunted Fiend what this might be admir'd,
> Admir'd, not fear'd; God and his Son except,
> Created thing naught vallu'd he nor shun'd;
> And with disdainful look thus first began. (II. 677–80)

'The line-endings', says Dr. Davie, 'are so far from being dramatically significant that Milton seems to have gone perversely out of his way to eliminate all that might be suspenseful. Inversion of word-order answers the question of what the Fiend "admir'd", before we have the chance to ask it. If we had been made to wait for the object of "admir'd" until after admiration had been distinguished from fear and the distinction elaborated on, a powerful suspense would have been built up. Instead the narrative run is halted while the distinction is laboriously made in a parenthesis which has all the distracting inertness of a footnote.'

The vigour of Dr. Davie's style should not disguise the oddity of what he is saying. 'What this might be' does not really *answer* 'the question of what the Fiend "admir'd" before we have the chance to ask it', because it is not an answer—it deliberately withholds any reassuring identification of the terrible shape. Satan does not, any more than we, know what faces him; but, whatever it might be, his superb courage is such that he is struck only with wonder and not fear. The distinction which to Dr. Davie has the 'inertness of a footnote' has to me the calm of supreme courage. 'Inert' will of course do as a description, provided we find it heroic that at such a moment Satan is inert, unmoved, *undaunted*—that he can command the imperturbability of a 'disdainful look'. 'Hell trembled', but Satan did not.

Indeed, the suspense is maintained just because we *are* in a vital sense 'made to wait for the object of "admir'd" '. The developing syntax may offer 'what this might be', but that only brings home how terrifyingly the 'object' remains undefined, and our feelings are hardly set at rest. Certainly the lines have poise—the poise is that of Satan. This is clear when these calm lines are set in their context, following immediately on lines very different in style: the hectic, elusive, spilling phantasmagoria that introduces Death.[1] To come on this poise after what has just preceded it, is to feel the full weight of 'what this might be', and the full weight of Satan's courage. So perhaps the narrative run is not halted but suspended—and creates suspense.

If Dr. Davie's examples fail to convince, then the third part of his essay becomes an interesting irrelevance, since it is concerned to explain how this weakness of syntax came about, and to relate it to Milton's larger deficiency in narrative—his creation of an encyclopaedia instead of a poem. But Dr. Davie very properly forces us to look closely at the syntax. It seems to me that here Milton achieves the elevated dignity of his Grand Style without sacrificing sense and sensitivity.

IV. THE UNSUCCESSFUL METAPHOR

Milton's syntax can in most cases be defended—it is not wilful or merely magniloquent. But when we turn to the place of metaphor in the Grand Style, more has to be conceded to the anti-Miltonists. It seems true that Milton's style is not very metaphorical, and that this is in some ways a pity. 'The greatest thing by far is to be a master of metaphor', said Aristotle, and most critics have concurred. But modern critics seem often to talk as if metaphor were the only source of poetic power and beauty. Though Milton certainly does not show Shakespearian fertility of metaphor, he creates similar effects by other means. Perhaps the effects that I am to consider as part of the Grand Style and of Milton's delicate subtlety could be called in some sense metaphorical. But it is wiser to grant the point.

[1] Quoted on p. 39 above.

Not, of course, that it should surprise us that Milton's Grand Style is seldom metaphorical. Apparently the same is true of Homer and Virgil. The very nature of the epic will discourage metaphor—or at any rate those metaphors whose boldness we find attractive elsewhere but which would seem pert or distracting in *Paradise Lost*. The metaphorical richness of Shakespeare admittedly defeats all argument, but the metaphors of, say, Donne or Hopkins flourish in poems that dramatize a moment rather than tell a gigantic story. The skills and beauty of the epic poet will be those of the long-distance runner, rather than of the boxer. Our pleasure will not be that of surprise, of jolt and jerk, but of anticipation and of suspense, felicities controlled by larger rhythms. It is not an accident that Hopkins should have chosen for an effect he admired the word *explode*.[1] Explosion, fusion—such are the terms in which modern criticism rightly praises a certain kind of effect. But the vitality in Milton's style will not be that of a bomb, but rather that of a scent, active and beautiful both as a harbinger and as a memory. Anticipations, echoes, reminders: all these exist in *Paradise Lost* not only in explicit narrative and action, but also take a local habitation.

In a later section I shall consider the kind of metaphor which Milton used in *Paradise Lost* aptly and beautifully. And in a later chapter I shall discuss another famous success, the epic similes. Though Milton did not merely *follow* the traditions of the epic simile, he did find a congenial tradition here, a chance to be original with the minimum of alteration. It seems to me that he always needed some such tradition, whether one of etymology (the source of his success in metaphor), or of epic practice (the source of his success in simile). The comparative failure in metaphor which is the subject of this section seems to occur when there is no such tradition, when the kind of metaphor or simile is one which springs only and entirely from immediate imagination and wits. Certainly Milton's language is novel, but its novelty is released incessantly from existing materials and traditions.

[1] *The Letters of Hopkins to Robert Bridges*, ed. C. C. Abbott (1935), p. 90.

I am not arguing for the superiority of either sort of novelty; but in the use of metaphor it seems that Milton (unlike Shakespeare) could not often encompass both sorts.

Mr. Eliot has praised Milton's 'inerrancy, conscious or unconscious, in writing so as to make the best display of his talents, and the best concealment of his weaknesses'.[1] This inerrancy is greatest in *Paradise Lost* (though even there it is naturally not total). Which means that the kind of metaphor which I may for brevity call Shakespearian hardly appears at all. A weakness, or more truly a limitation, of the style is rightly tacit. But fully to understand the Grand Style in its strength and limitations we should not leave the matter there, so I turn to *Samson Agonistes*. Here Milton was provoked by dramatic tradition to embark mistakenly on the Shakespearian type of metaphor. It is here that the Grand Style passes from a scarcity of metaphor to a disappointing failure in metaphor.

It was Dr. Johnson who first made this objection to *Samson Agonistes*: 'sometimes metaphors find admission, even where their consistency is not accurately preserved. Thus Samson confounds loquacity with a shipwreck.'[2]

> How could I once look up, or heave the head,
> Who like a foolish Pilot have shipwrack't,
> My Vessel trusted to me from above,
> Gloriously rigg'd; and for a word, a tear,
> Fool, have divulg'd the secret gift of God . . . (197–201)

The weakness of the metaphor or simile here, as Johnson saw, is that Samson is like a bad pilot only in the respect that he has carelessly shipwrecked—loquacity has nothing to do with it. Pilots don't shipwreck because they divulge secrets. To complain that the consistency of the metaphor is not accurately preserved is not mere neo-classical pedantry, since metaphor—like all poetic effects—is not isolated but lives along the line. If the line is broken, then the metaphor may die. And the way in which the sentence about the pilot

[1] 'Milton II.' *On Poetry and Poets*, p. 155.

[2] *The Rambler*, No. 140 (20 July 1751).

unrolls, the punctuation (semicolon) and the continuation through *and*, all these bring about a situation in which Milton is, within the same sentence, asking us both to take his metaphor with tragic seriousness, and then to ignore it. If we are not to find the effect inconsistent, we must quite ignore the pilot when we reach the secret—it is not merely that the secret makes no real addition to the metaphor, but that they are positively incompatible. Instead of the light being that of the sun, it is merely electric. The metaphor is switched on for a few seconds, and then switched off.

The same Johnsonian objection might be made to the beginning of this speech by Samson, when he tells how he has learned

> How counterfeit a coin they are who friends
> Bear in their Superscription (of the most
> I would be understood) in prosperous days
> They swarm, but in adverse withdraw their head . . . (189–92)

The image of the coin, which 'Superscription' asks us to take seriously, turns within the same sentence into a swarm of something (summer flies, presumably, but where they appear from is not clear), who then *withdraw their head*—a phrase which can only dubiously be applied to a swarm and which moreover is unhelpfully apt to a coin, which has a head but cannot withdraw it.

Such blurring of the metaphors is not at all the same sort of thing as Shakespearian fertility. If Shakespeare's metaphors are 'mixed', the mixing is itself a source of new meaning. That a 'new-born babe' would not normally be thought to 'stride' is exactly the point in those famous lines of Macbeth's: suddenly we see the astonishing strength of what we can mistakenly see as only fragile and defenceless. 'Or to take arms against a sea of troubles' is a better line than would be a tidier neo-classical version ('Or to take arms against a siege of troubles'), but not because mixed metaphors don't matter. Shakespeare's line, just because in a flash it mentions a man taking up arms against a sea, presents more accurately the tragic hopelessness of what Hamlet is invoking.

And Milton elsewhere is often a master of such meaningful incongruities.[1] Our horrified wonder at the fallen angels is elicited by the grotesqueness of a multitude which pours from *frozen* loins:

> A multitude, like which the populous North
> Pour'd never from her frozen loyns . . . (*P.L.*, i. 351–2)

How feeble in comparison is the dull straightforwardness of Du Bartas:

> the *Goth*, who whilom issuing forth
> From the cold, frozen Ilands of the North.[2]

Naturally Bentley found Milton's enigma intolerable: 'The Diction is faulty: *Frozen Loins* are improper for Populousness.'[3] And Pearce had nothing to say, and presumably hoped that mere geography would save him: 'I think that the word *loyns*, tho' *frozen* be the Epithet, may pass with a less scrupulous Reader.'[4] But of course the phrase is 'improper for Populousness'—and so all the more apt to the devils. As Mrs. I. G. MacCaffrey says, ' "frozen loyns" is a kind of horrible parody on one of his favorite ideas, the fertility that comes from God and from God's symbol, the sun.'[5]

But if metaphors are mixed, not in order to carve new meaning, but through perfunctoriness, then the verse must suffer. And it is hard to see what relevant defence could be made of the blurring in Samson's coin and swarm.

It will hardly do, for example, to claim that it isn't the coin which swarms, but the friends. True, but there is something wrong with a metaphor in the course of which we have to switch back abruptly to the tenor of what is said. The coin ought to embody the friends so completely that there would be no question of our having to say at one moment 'These words refer to the coin', and at another 'These refer to the friends'.

[1] See pp. 14–16 above.
[2] Sylvester's *Works*, ed. A. B. Grosart (1880), i. 147.
[3] p. 17. [4] p. 30. [5] *P.L. as 'Myth'* (1959), p. 129.

The famous swarm of hornets in the very first speech of the play seems to me as disappointing, since the sentence rushes forward to something incongruous. If we give it our full attention, it does not become incongruously meaningful, but merely odd:

> restless thoughts, that like a deadly swarm
> Of Hornets arm'd, no sooner found alone,
> But rush upon me thronging, and present
> Times past, what once I was, and what am now. (19–22)

The main question is how hornets can possibly 'present times past, what once I was, and what am now'. Plainly hornets can do no such thing, and at this point we are to think only of the 'restless thoughts'. But the hornets are there at 'thronging', and it is only a comma and the word *and* that separates them from 'times past'. We are asked at one moment to feel the full weight of Samson's suffering through the deadly hornets, and then immediately to forget about them. Of course it is not difficult to protect the last line from absurdity—all you have to do is forget about the hornets. But that means forgetting Samson's sufferings, since it is the hornets which have presented them to our imagination. Raleigh said of mixed metaphors in *Paradise Lost*: 'He trusts the reader to follow his thought without grammatical readjustment—to drop the symbol and remember only the thing symbolised.'[1] But there is something odd in the idea that a poet can so casually 'drop the symbol' he has been using. Milton never does so when he is using the sort of metaphor or simile which suits his gifts.

Metaphors and similes used in this way are bound to lack authority, since they are not inseparable from their context. Another metaphor could be substituted, and the lines around it would not have to be altered. Since the last dozen words of Milton's sentence have nothing to do with hornets, then the sentence itself is not a living tissue. And the metaphor, which has been slotted in, can as easily be slotted out.

[1] *Milton*, p. 213.

What, for instance, happens to the *plant* in these lines?—lines which once again comprise the same sentence:

> Ordain'd thy nurture holy, as of a Plant;
> Select, and Sacred, Glorious for a while,
> The miracle of men: then in an hour
> Ensnar'd, assaulted, overcome, led bound. (362–5)

We are asked to give the weight of our imaginations to the plant until the colon. And then the plant is made to disappear. At any rate, if we don't agree to let it disappear (to let it means that our attachment to it can never have been very strong), we are left with the inconsistency of a *plant*'s being 'Ensnar'd, assaulted, overcome, led bound'. It is interesting that when Mr. Stein[1] wishes to quote with emphasis this speech of Manoah, he finds it best to begin at 'Select, and Sacred, Glorious for a while'. Leaving out the plant does remove the inconsistency of 'Ensnar'd . . .'—but at the cost of obscuring the emblematic allusion in 'Glorious for a while'.

Moreover, this disappointingly afflicts even the most nearly successful of Milton's similes in this poem. Samson condemns Dalila,

> who shore me
> Like a tame Weather, all my precious fleece,
> Then turn'd me out ridiculous, despoil'd,
> Shav'n, and disarm'd among my enemies. (537–40)

This builds up admirably through *shore*, *tame Weather*, *precious fleece*, and *shav'n*; and then—'Shav'n, and disarm'd among my enemies'. At which the image completely collapses. (By which I don't mean that the poet fails to continue it, but that he contradicts it.) With the first word of the line, *Shav'n*, one must still take the metaphor with tragic seriousness (and very good it is). With the third word, *disarm'd*, one must have entirely forgotten it—if not the word is ridiculous. It is not merely that a sheep is in no sense whatever disarmed

[1] *Heroic Knowledge* (1957), p. 149.

by being shorn. It is not merely that a sheep is one of the most harmless and least armed of animals, so that in fighting terms what Dalila did is particularly irrelevant. No, the real trouble is that Milton has felt bound to stress the tameness of this unarmed animal. It is not even an ordinary sheep, but a tame wether. The simile, which is apt in so many ways, is virtually annihilated when Milton 'drops the symbol', abandons the sheep, and leaves us only with Samson, 'disarm'd among my enemies'.

It might be claimed that such passages do not much matter, since there are so very few metaphors and similes in *Samson Agonistes*. But, on the contrary, this is just why they are important. The abstract austerity of their setting insists that they carry a great deal of imaginative weight. But not only is there a sad lack of control in the explicit figures such as have been mentioned, but there are even fewer figures than there ought to be. By which I mean that phrases like 'seal of silence' or 'give the reins', which ought to be metaphorical, are used here by Milton with a feebleness that keeps them merely words.

Nothing in the context puts any life into the phrase 'give the reins' when Manoah declares:

> What windy joy this day had I conceiv'd
> Hopeful of his Delivery, which now proves
> Abortive as the first-born bloom of spring
> Nipt with the lagging rear of winters frost.
> Yet e're I give the reins to grief, say first,
> How dy'd he? death to life is crown or shame.
> All by him fell thou say'st, by whom fell he,
> What glorious hand gave Samson his deaths wound? (1574–81)

Dead metaphors of this kind are very different from those which lie in words like 'transport'.[1] Such words plainly have metaphors lurking in them, and it is an added beauty if a poet can use this as a source of strength. But so much of language is made up of dead metaphors, in this sense, that

[1] See p. 59 below.

we could hardly expect even the most alert of poets to be continually refreshing them. Dr. Davie, who has done most to clarify and illustrate the invigoration of dead metaphor, has an apt warning:

> The right strategy is not to reveal the metaphor, the concretion, in every word used, even in prepositions like 'upon' or 'outside'. This is the strategy of some poets writing today; and the result is only an incessant and intolerable fidget. If all the words we use are dead or dormant metaphors, then in any one poem the poet must permit the greater part of such words to continue sleeping or shamming dead. Only in that way can he bring into prominence the metaphors he has for the moment selected to create or to re-create.[1]

But it is not possible to defend Milton's use of 'give the reins' by such an appeal. Or take the word *flower*. We ought to resist the imaginative withering which results if we entirely cut off the literal meaning of the word from its application as 'the best, the élite'. Granted, if a poet fails to invigorate a dead metaphor, his writing is not necessarily slack. It merely shows in this one respect less vigour than another poet might have achieved. Take the word 'flourish', separate from 'flower'. Milton brings them together:

> Roses, and Gessamin
> Rear'd high thir flourisht heads. (*P.L.*, IV. 698–9)

But we could hardly complain if he used 'flourish' with simple straightforwardness.

Yet 'flower' is bound to suggest primarily a beautiful and transitory plant—the word refers directly to something which we know and see all the time, and a poet is taking a great risk if he insists on taking no notice at all of what is so obvious, direct, and suggestive a meaning.

It is one thing when Milton's editor, Thomas Newton, uses the word (as any of us feebly might) as no more than an empty synonym for 'the best': 'besides the flower of those which have been already published, here are several new observations'. But it is another thing when we find Milton

[1] *Articulate Energy*, p. 134.

using the word in the same way, when we find that for a moment Milton is writing with no more power than Newton:

> Then with what trivial weapon came to hand,
> The Jaw of a dead Ass, his sword of bone,
> A thousand fore-skins fell, the flower of Palestin
> In Ramath-lechi famous to this day. (142–5)

That the word is feeble there becomes clear if we notice how these lines are thoroughly paraphrased by Samson when he tells how he

> with a trivial weapon fell'd
> Thir choicest youth. (263–4)

What *flower* can really mean when we apply it to a person was unforgettably shown in *Paradise Lost*:

> Proserpin gathring flours
> Her self a fairer Floure by gloomie Dis
> Was gatherd . . . (IV. 269–71)

Or Eve, 'Her self, though fairest unsupported Flour' (IX. 432). Such a way of using words is disappointingly distant from making the Messenger tell how the roof fell

> Upon the heads of all who sate beneath,
> Lords, Ladies, Captains, Councellors, or Priests,
> Thir choice nobility and flower, not only
> Of this but each Philistian City round
> Met from all parts to solemnize this Feast. (1652–6)

'City' and 'met' ensure that the word 'flower' is dead.

In all such instances flower means no more than might cream. The verse would not be much affected if instead of flower we read cream. And my disappointment is proportionate to the distance that there is in fact between a flower and cream.

So that the critic who is not unhappy would have to say that the complete separation of the two meanings of 'flower' was not undesirable, and that there are in effect two separate words. But is there nothing at all inept about the phrase that Tennyson's Grandmother uses of her Willy: that he was 'the flower of the flock'?

When, very occasionally, Milton in *Paradise Lost* was lured into using the kind of metaphor which suited neither his great gifts nor his great traditions, he was liable to be reproved by Bentley. So that when Eve was described,

> her Heav'nly forme
> Angelic, but more soft, and Feminine, (IX. 457–8)

Bentley was contemptuous: '*Eve*'s Form it seems was *Angelic*, not in Metaphor, but in Reality: for that's the Affair here. So we must suppose, she had six Wings, as *Raphael* had.' And, remembering Milton's insistence on the 'liquid texture' of the angelic substance, he added that 'if *Eve* had been more *soft*, more *feminine*, than such were; she would have been no fit Mate for her Husband'.[1] Pearce tried to escape: 'Why may not *Angelic* be spoken Metaphorically, as well as *Heavenly*, which certainly is so?'[2] But it is a thin idea of metaphor which supposes that it need make less sense than a statement does, and Mr. Empson rightly protested that 'we ought not to have to be fobbed off when there are live walking metaphors just round the corner'.[3] There are few live walking metaphors in *Samson Agonistes*, as Dr. Johnson insisted. Milton's gifts were not suited to this kind of metaphor. His true poetry is created out of ancient materials, as in a foundry—not spun out of his own entrails as by a spider. But in *Paradise Lost* Milton succeeds not only in the epic similes but also in other effects which are in some measure metaphorical, and are in any case powerfully alive.

V. THE SUCCESSFUL METAPHOR

The dignity of the epic is not compatible with such metaphors as are boldly and explosively new. But there is more than one kind of verbal life, and both his temperament and his respect for literary decorum impelled Milton to choose to bring ancient metaphors back to life rather than to forge new ones. The magnificent powers of Donne and Hopkins are

[1] p. 284. [2] p. 315. [3] *Some Versions*, p. 154.

sometimes in danger of making us silently assume that all our respect should go to the pioneer and none to the historian. Sometimes it even seems to be implied that it is only the pioneer who is 'sincere'. But each has value, and each has his apt style. Milton, like all epic poets, is concerned mainly to lead us back, not to blaze new trails. And the vigour of his words is a matter of his leading us back to the riches buried in them.

At its simplest, such a use of language does no more (and no less) than make words mean what they ought to mean. Dr. Davie has pointed out how often the verbal activity of the eighteenth-century poets is a matter of bringing dead metaphors to life. The poet takes a word or a phrase which has become slack or empty, and puts it into a context which suddenly brings back to life the original force. So any of us can now talk of 'goading' someone into a fury—but it is for Pope to say how his wit will 'goad the prelate slumbering in his stall', where the double aptness of *stall* (to prelate and to ox) tautens the whole line and puts the sting back into *goad*. Such a use of words might be thought to be particularly the method of those who seek to be original with the minimum of alteration—but it is very common in Milton, and ought to remind us of the balance between his notable idiosyncrasy of style and his observance of decorum. His admiration for the traditional is as much a matter of language as of epic machinery or convention.

Milton's Grand Style, in other words, has something in common with Goldsmith as well as with Hopkins. Dr. Davie points out how 'Goldsmith enlivens the metaphor gone dead in the locution "smiling land" ' (where smiling is 'beautiful', as in the Latin *ridere*):

> While scourg'd by famine from the smiling land,
> The mournful peasant leads his humble band

—where the land is 'seen to smile with heartless indifference on the ruined peasant'.[1] But Milton, too, had seen the ominous

[1] *The Deserted Village*, lines 299–300; *Purity of Diction in English Verse* (1952), pp. 50–51.

possibilities in the beautiful convention of the 'smiling' of nature. It is explicit in Eve's words after the Fall:

> for see the Morn,
> All unconcern'd with our unrest, begins
> Her rosie progress smiling. (XI. 173–5)[1]

And it is implicit at that earlier tragic moment when Adam's faltering heart divines the ill which Eve is to conceal under a blithe countenance:

> by the Tree
> Of Knowledge he must pass, there he her met,
> Scarse from the Tree returning; in her hand
> A bough of fairest fruit that downie smil'd. (IX. 848–51)

Once again the smile is 'all unconcern'd with our unrest', or (in Dr. Davie's words) one of 'heartless indifference'. And once again the metaphor is enlivened, without shock and with the dignity suited to the Grand Style.

The metaphor is usually faded, too, when *transport* is given the extended sense of 'to carry away with emotion'. In Milton's hands, indeed in any poet's, it often might seem to mean no more than 'with one's emotions out of control'. But Milton re-establishes the power of the original metaphor, by setting the word in a context which stresses the physical roots of the emotional meaning, so that we see a *transport* as something that does literally and powerfully *move* you. So it is when God sees Satan 'coasting the wall of Heav'n':

> Onely begotten Son, seest thou what rage
> Transports our adversarie, whom no bounds
> Prescrib'd, no barrs of Hell, nor all the chains
> Heapt on him there, nor yet the main Abyss
> Wide interrupt can hold; so bent he seems
> On desperat revenge, that shall redound
> Upon his own rebellious head. And now
> Through all restraint broke loose he wings his way
> Not farr off Heav'n . . . (III. 80–88)

God at this moment is not concerned primarily with Satan's emotions, but with the desperate physical energy of

[1] There is a similar effect at V. 122–4.

his journey. And the whole passage is superbly expressive of such energy. In diction: 'broke loose he wings his way'. And in syntax: notice how the crucial verb *can hold* flies triumphantly free, at the very end of its clause, from the grip of the previous twenty-two words of heaped chains. It is the superb syntax of 'can hold' which is prior to, and the condition of, the lines' magnificent sound which Mr. Empson praised.[1]

The result of these effects is that when God says

> seest thou what rage
> Transports our adversarie,

the words compress his knowledge of Satan's single motive with his observation of his escape from Hell. After all, it is literally true that rage *transports* Satan.

This may seem over-ingenious, but there is substantiation in another famous passage where once again the powerful physical meaning reinforces the emotional one—emotion itself being a form of motion. Satan is entranced by the beauty of Eve, and for a moment he stands abstracted from his own evil. Then,

> Thoughts, *whither have ye led me*, with what sweet
> Compulsion thus *transported* to forget
> What *hither brought us* . . . (IX. 473–5)

Surely the italicized sequence insists on our taking 'transported' as very much more than a synonym for 'out of control'. And 'compulsion', too, renews its original *drive*.

That Milton was particularly fond of this complex of ideas is clear from Adam's tribute to Eve, when 'transported', 'commotion', and 'unmov'd' all renew their original movement:

> But here
> Farr otherwise, transported I behold,
> Transported touch; here passion first I felt,
> Commotion strange, in all enjoyments else
> Superiour and unmov'd. (VIII. 528–32)

[1] *Milton's God*, p. 119.

The words have a similar unobtrusive and dignified energy when, during the temptation of Eve, Satan is described as 'the spirited sly Snake' (IX. 613). Obviously the main meaning is 'possessed by a spirit', for which the *O.E.D.* quotes the phrase. And spirited is used elsewhere in the poem to mean exactly that (III. 717). But the other meaning ('brisk, blithe') is not left out. Plainly the meanings co-exist in a synonym like 'animated', and Milton is taking advantage of both of them. The very next mention of the snake describes it as 'the wilie Adder, blithe and glad', *spirited* in the modern sense. And the 'evil Spirit' returns explicitly in the simile which follows, that of the *ignis fatuus*.

The degeneration of the transcendent brightness of Satan to that of a will-of-the-wisp is summed up in the way that Milton uses the word 'glory'. By stressing the sense of 'brightness, halo', he makes it clear that there is no true glory except that of God's goodness, and that Satan has only what—in a superbly shrivelling phrase—he calls 'permissive glory' (X. 451),[1] that is, 'false glitter'. We need to see the halo in the *glory* of the famous lines on Satan:

> his form had yet not lost
> All her Original brightness, nor appear'd
> Less then Arch Angel ruind, and th' excess
> Of Glory obscur'd: As when the Sun new ris'n
> Looks through the Horizontal misty Air
> Shorn of his Beams . . . (I. 591–6)[2]

There the context all bears on *glory*, insisting that it is literal as well as moral. So it is too when Beelzebub despairs of 'all our Glory extinct' (I. 141). It was Patrick Hume, in 1695, who made the apt comment: 'put out, as a Flame, or any thing that burns and shines, a word well expressing the loss of that Angelick Beauty, which like a Glory attended on their Innocency, which by their foul Rebellion they had forfeited.... *Extinctus* is used in the same Metaphorical manner by *Virgil*.'[3]

1 For a similar effect compare 'Forc't Halleluiahs' (II. 243).

2 Cleanth Brooks analyses this passage, 'Milton and the New Criticism', *Sewanee Review* (1951).

3 *Poetical Works of Milton, Annotations by P.H.* (1695), p. 11.

It was the eighteenth-century editors who grasped the nature of the style, perhaps because the eighteenth-century poets owed so much to it. (The poets who merely imitated it are another and sadder matter.) Jonathan Richardson insisted that Milton's 'Sense is Crouded So Close, that Those who have been us'd to be indulg'd with Words and Sentences to Play withall, will find no Such Here; they must Attend Diligently, or Somthing Material will pass away'.[1]

So when we hear that the heathen gods 'with their darkness durst *affront* his light' (I. 391), Richardson brings out the force: 'This Word Carries a Stronger Sense than what is Commonly intended by it, though it also has That; it is from the *Italian Affrontare*, to Meet Face to Face; an Impudent Braving.'[2]

'Front' is still used by Milton in the sense of forehead, face to face; and the 'Stronger Sense' returns when Eve—as often—makes explicit what the poet had elsewhere muted. Her confidence rings with too emphatic a set of repetitions when she says that it will not matter even if the devil does tempt her:

> onely our Foe
> Tempting affronts us with his foul esteem
> Of our integritie: his foul esteeme
> Sticks no dishonor on our Front, but turns
> Foul on himself. (IX. 327–31)

There one can notice the precision which the word 'integrity' still had. For Milton it really does mean completeness, unity, wholeness—just as the word *whole* has the same root as the word holy. 'Our integritie': it is that innocent unity which Eve breaks when she wilfully withdraws her hand from her husband's. In the same way, when Satan corrupts the angels in Heaven, Milton brings out the full force of integrity by setting it against 'ambiguous': Satan

> casts between
> Ambiguous words and jealousies, to sound
> Or taint integritie . . . (V. 699–701)

[1] p. clxvii. [2] p. 29.

Such mastery of the context does more than anything else can to invigorate language while still preserving decorum.

The inspiration of words that would otherwise be half-dead is inseparable from Milton's famous liking for using words with their original Latin meaning. Of course one must first put aside those 'Latinisms' which are no more than completely normal seventeenth-century English (say, *admire* as 'wonder at'); and then concentrate on what seem acts of choice by Milton. Sometimes a Miltonic usage may be of extreme rarity, and the question is simple. At other times, his deviation may be slight; but one should not put aside as critically irrelevant those moments when he seems to prefer what was apparently by then an unusual or a less usual application. Any critic is in danger of finding unique beauty in what was a casual or common usage; but any linguist is in danger of implying that in the past everybody wrote equally well.

Milton's Latinate usages are curiously open both to Mark Pattison's irrelevant praise (reading Milton as 'the last reward of consummated scholarship'), and to Dr. Leavis's equally irrelevant blame ('a callousness to the intrinsic nature of English'). Everything depends, as usual, on the particular case; on whether there is anything gained, in terms of meaning as well as sound, by his choosing to be Latinate. Is he simply being pedantic? Landor commented darkly, 'He soon begins to give the learned and less obvious signification to English words'.[1]

The extra meaning which Milton finds comes clearly from the fact that he does not discard the English meaning. As Raleigh said, 'He was not content to revive the exact classical meaning in place of the vague or weak English acceptation; he often kept both senses, and loaded the word with two meanings at once.'[2] What we have is not a pompous substitution, or an antiquarian delight in a remoter meaning, but an addition to the meaning, sometimes one of emphasis, sometimes one of refinement. Such Anglo-Latinisms are not

[1] *Works*, ed. Welby, v. 238.

[2] *Milton*, p. 209.

the property of Milton alone, and often they are simple enough. So every schoolboy knows that when Satan falls 'With hideous ruine and combustion down' (I. 46), *ruine* includes the literal falling of the Latin. Or that when the reed for the gunpowder is described as 'pernicious with one touch to fire' (VI. 520), *pernicious* is both 'destructive' and 'swift'.

But the effect can be much subtler. Dr. Davie's point about metaphor was anticipated by Thomas Newton in 1749, in commenting on the moment when Satan and the other devils turn into serpents:

> His Armes clung to his Ribs, his Leggs entwining
> Each other, till *supplanted* down he fell. (X. 512–13)

'We may observe here', said Newton, 'a singular beauty and elegance in Milton's language, and that is his using words in their strict and litteral sense, which are commonly apply'd to a metaphorical meaning, whereby he gives peculiar force to his expressions, and the litteral meaning appears more new and striking than the metaphor itself. We have an instance of this in the word *supplanted*, which is deriv'd from the Latin *supplanto*, to trip up one's heels or overthrow . . . and there are abundance of other examples in several parts of this work, but let it suffice to have taken notice of it here once for all.'[1]

This is a very fine critical comment, but it is perhaps not explicit enough as to why Milton here uses *supplanted* with its physical meaning. The applied moral meaning is in the background, and provides the grim irony with which Satan is always seen—Satan, on whom always evil 'recoils', on whose head revenge 'redounds'. Satan is the great supplanter: 'He set upon our fyrst parentes in paradyse, and by pride supplanted them' (More, 1522).[2] In *Paradise Regained* (IV. 607), too,

[1] ii. 252. Compare Arnold Stein on the release of the original metaphor in 'By Haralds voice *explain'd*': 'compared with the more primitive meaning, the derived meaning tends to be abstract, the accepted equivalent of the familiar result or even process of an action, but with no physical or imaginative sense of the very happening of that process' (*Answerable Style*, p. 147).

[2] *O.E.D.* 2: 'To cause to fall', from 1340. It also cites *c.* 1610, *Women Saints*: 'The divell envying these her vertuous studies, thought to supplant her.'

the word itself reminds us of this. So 'supplanted' here is a succinct and telling comment on the reason for Satan's being overthrown (hoist with his own petard), at the very same moment as it tells us that he *was* overthrown:

> Immediate are the Acts of God, more swift
> Then time or motion, but to human ears
> Cannot without process of speech be told. (VII. 176–8)

Milton's process of speech is so compact that it can even reflect divine immediacy, the divine moment that instantaneously judges crime *and* punishment. Milton's phrase has what Raphael, in an excellent phrase, called 'Speed almost Spiritual'.

An equally acute comment by Newton (expanding a note by Hume) brings home that Milton's reaching down to the roots is certainly not limited to Latinisms. During the council in Hell, Beelzebub yearns to destroy God's

> whole Creation, or possess
> All as our own, and drive as we were driven,
> The punie habitants. (II. 365–7)

Hume's gloss ran: 'The weak infirm Possessors, the late made Inmates of this new World: *Puisné*, born since, created long since us, Angelick Beings boasting Eternity.'[1] And Newton developed the point: 'It is possible that the author by *puny* might mean no more than weak or little; but yet if we reflect how frequently he uses words in their proper and primary signification, it seems probable that he might include likewise the sense of the French (from whence it is deriv'd) *puis né*, born since, created long after us.'[2] Again it is only a matter of making more explicit the double meaning which Hume and Newton so admirably fasten on. That Man was 'born since' the fallen angels is precisely the great reason why they hate him. The hatred and its cause were clear

[1] p. 65.

[2] i. 105. The survival of the form 'puisne' make a ready awareness of the derivation of *puny* likely. Moreover, the seventeenth-century sense of 'junior' will have pointed towards Milton's usage.

enough from the way in which Beelzebub introduced the subject of Man in this same speech:

> some new Race call'd Man, about this time
> To be created like to us, though less
> In power and excellence, but favour'd more
> Of him who rules above. (II. 348–51)

The mixture of envy and contempt comes out in the bitter placing of 'less' and 'more'. And the same feelings stir Satan to cry out against

> this new Favorite
> Of Heav'n, this Man of Clay, Son of despite,
> Whom us the more to spite his Maker rais'd
> From dust: spite then with spite is best repaid.[1]

That men are 'the punie habitants', then, superbly compresses Beelzebub's contemptuous reasons for hating them (new favourites) *and* his reasons for revenge: they are weak. To the fallen angels, men are weak just because they are a sort of divine afterthought, a poor attempt, to make up the numbers in Heaven. The comment of Hume and Newton on this one word radiates into the whole of the poem—a mark of good criticism and of a great poem.

VI. WORD-PLAY

With words like *supplanted* and *punie* we have perhaps moved across the invisible line that separates the vivified metaphor from word-play. Not that classifications much matter; what is important is to understand exactly what Milton is saying when he uses such words. It is only rarely that decorum permits Milton's word-play in *Paradise Lost* to have the brusque simplicity which we associate with the word 'pun'.

'It appears then on record that the first overt crime of the refractory angels was *punning*: they fell rapidly after that.'[2] Landor is here being grimly contemptuous of the most

[1] IX. 175–8. Cp. II. 834 and IX. 147–9.

[2] *Works*, ed. Welby, v. 258.

obvious puns in the poem, those of the artillery during the war in Heaven:

> But that I doubt, however witness Heaven,
> Heav'n witness thou anon, while we discharge
> Freely our part: yee who appointed stand
> Do as you have in charge, and briefly touch
> What we propound, and loud that all may hear . . .
> (VI. 563–7)

Unlike some of the eighteenth-century editors, Landor's objection was not that punning is indecorous in a religious epic, but that it was poor punning: 'the wit . . . is worthy of newly-made devils who never had heard any before, and falls as foul on the poetry as on the antagonist.'

Addison had put the same point of view: 'This Passage I look upon to be the most exceptionable in the whole Poem, as being nothing else but a String of Puns, and those too very indifferent ones.'[1] Yet the crudity at this point is perhaps dramatically apt, as some eighteenth-century commentators argued.[2] Fortunately, though, a defence of Milton's word-play has stronger ground than the war in Heaven, even when the aim of the word-play is the same: contempt.

Of the five phrases which Addison deplored in *The Spectator* (No. 297), four signify contempt (or self-contempt): Milton's, in *that small infantry* (I. 575); Satan's, in

> begirt th' Almighty Throne
> Beseeching or besieging (V. 865–6),

as well as in 'which tempted our attempt' (I. 642), and in 'At one slight bound high overleap'd all bound' (IV. 181).

Addison's other example had a more sombre ring: 'That brought into this World a world of woe' (IX. 11). But whatever the tone of such word-play, he had no doubt of its

[1] *The Spectator*, No. 279 (19 Jan. 1712).

[2] Richardson, Thyer, and Gillies. E. E. Kellett put the points well in 'The Puns in Milton', *London Quarterly and Holborn Review* (1934), 6th ser., iii. 469–76. Hume (pp. 204–5) is still the most helpful editor as to how many puns there are; he points out not only *overture, discharge*, &c., but also *result* ('to Skip back'), and *composition* ('compounded Nitre and Sulphur').

inappropriateness: 'I know there are figures for this kind of speech, that some of the greatest ancients have been guilty of it, and that Aristotle himself has given it a place in his Rhetoric among the beauties of that art. But as it is in itself poor and trifling, it is, I think, at present universally exploded by all the masters of polite writing.'

The other eighteenth-century commentators concurred,[1] and Dr. Johnson (for whom a 'punster' was a 'low wit, who endeavours at reputation by double meaning') included word-play in his massive summing-up: 'His play on words, in which he delights too often; his equivocations, which Bentley endeavours to defend by the example of the ancients; his unnecessary and ungraceful use of terms of art, it is not necessary to mention, because they are easily remarked and generally censured, and at last bear so little proportion to the whole that they scarcely deserve the attention of a critick.'[2]

Yet Milton is just as aware as Johnson of how carefully word-play must be used in a religious epic. All of which makes it natural that in Milton's Grand Style the most common sort of word-play should be that which insists on the derivation of a word, and so expels the bizarre or the fortuitous. When Raleigh was discussing Milton's puns, he pointed out that 'it seems likely that he believed in an etymological relation between the two words, and so fancied that he was drawing attention to an original unity of meaning. Some such hypothesis is needful to mitigate the atrocity of his worst pun'[3]—i.e. the ravenous ravens. But Milton certainly was not alone in his etymological faith. Mr. Arnold Williams, in his study of the commentators on Genesis who were so important to Milton, has pointed out that they 'were the inheritors of a tradition stemming from Plato's *Cratylus*, according to which the etymology of the word gives a glimpse into the true nature of the thing'.[4]

[1] e.g., 'There are several Puns in the *Paradise Lost*, which are the grossest Faults in that Poem' (C. Falconer's *Essay upon Milton's Imitations of the Ancients*, 1741, p. 47).

[2] *Lives of the Poets*, ed. Hill, i. 188.

[3] *Milton*, p. 211.

[4] *The Common Expositor* (1948), p. 230.

Raleigh's comment, and his example of the ravens, were both taken up by Mr. Empson in a characteristically subtle and ranging argument, one which is particularly important in its bearing on the epic and its dignity: 'When a reader can see no similarity between the notions concerned, such as a derivation is likely to imply, the pun seems more trivial and to proceed from a less serious apprehension of the word's meaning.'[1]

Take, as an example of decorous power, the simple phrase *distance and distaste* in the opening lines of Book IX:

> No more of talk where God or Angel Guest
> With Man, as with his Friend, familiar us'd
> To sit indulgent, and with him partake
> Rural repast, permitting him the while
> Venial discourse unblam'd: I now must change
> Those Notes to Tragic; foul distrust, and breach
> Disloyal on the part of Man, revolt,
> And disobedience: On the part of Heav'n
> Now alienated, distance and distaste . . .

One's interest in the phrase is surely aroused by its alliterative crescendo; we rise with pauses through 'discourse . . . distrust . . . disloyal . . . disobedience' to the full clash of the cymbals in *distance and distaste*. Why the crescendo? Is it merely part of that Miltonic music, or is it directing our attention to meaning? We may remember Jonathan Richardson's insistence that 'whoever will Possess His Ideas must Dig for them, and Oftentimes pretty far below the Surface.'[2] Indeed, the clash is meant to draw our attention to the fact that here is somewhere to dig—it twitches in our hand.

To take *distance* first. One of the first things to strike us is the inexactness of the antithesis, 'on the part of Man . . . on the part of *Heav'n*'. Why not on the part of God? Then one notices that the next word—'On the part of Heav'n, now *alienated*'—is also a word that brings in *place*. The substitution of 'Heav'n' for 'God', and the sequence in 'now alienated, distance . . .', bring home that Milton is taking advantage of the literal life latent in the word *distance*. God

[1] *Seven Types of Ambiguity*, p. 104.

[2] p. cxliv.

must now be aloof and distant; and the force of this is increased by the pressure towards the literal meaning of distance. Heaven is a very long way from earth; before the Fall, that was of no matter; but the distance is now moral and spiritual, and not merely material. The distance is no longer no gap at all to the loving harmony of God and Man; and with the Fall of man, we see also the fall of language. Distance is no longer a neutral fact, but a 'just rebuke, and judgement giv'n'. God was distant, now he is *distant*.[1]

Such a reading is made plausible by the frequency with which Milton uses 'distance' for the literal miles from earth to Heaven. So Adam asks Raphael 'How first began this Heav'n which we behold / Distant so high' (VII. 86–87). And Raphael tells of his speed, in a passage which significantly relates the corporeal to the spiritual:

> his Omnipotence,
> That to corporeal substances could adde
> Speed almost Spiritual; mee thou thinkst not slow,
> Who since the Morning hour set out from Heav'n
> Where God resides, and ere mid-day arriv'd
> In Eden, distance inexpressible
> By Numbers that have name. (VIII. 108–14)

For as Raleigh said of Milton, 'All his greatest effects are achieved in the realm of the physical and moral sublime, where the moral relations are conditioned chiefly by the physical.'[2]

What, then, of *distaste*? Would things have been very different if instead of the distaste of Heaven we had been told of its 'disapproval' or its 'Divine displeasure' (IX. 993)? There does not at first seem to be much in the immediate context which will invigorate the metaphor in 'distaste'. But the pressure is not exerted only locally. It is exerted also by the countless times that the Fall is described as the *tasting* of the apple. The real structure of the phrase is of a brilliantly

[1] *O.E.D.*: 'OF. *destance* had the sense "discord, quarrel", which was also the earliest in English. . . . After 1600, passing into the sense of "estrangement, coolness".'

[2] *Milton*, p. 113.

unspoken pun. On the part of man, *taste*; on the part of Heaven, *distaste*.

Let me simply list *some* of the instances from Book IX alone—the whole story of the Fall is told in them:

> But of this Tree we may not taste nor touch . . .
> Goddess humane, reach then, and freely taste . . .
> . . . Forbids us then to taste . . .
> Fair to the Eye, inviting to the Taste . . .
> Eve, Intent now wholly on her taste . . .
> . . . a Tree of danger tasted . . .
> Thou therfore also taste . . .
> . . . foretasted Fruit . . .
> . . . Taste so Divine . . .
> On my experience, Adam, freely taste . . .
> Eve, now I see thou art exact of taste . . .[1]

These are nothing like all the examples from Book IX alone, as a glance at the concordance will show. (In fact, the word and its variants come about thirty times in this Book alone.)

But it might still be argued that such ruthless and relentless pressure on 'taste' is not enough to affect Heaven's *distaste*. So one looks again to the context at the beginning of Book IX. And at this point one sees how important it is to take *distance and distaste* as a unit, since only then can we appreciate how horrifyingly far we have come from the bliss of Paradise—from the time when God or Angel with Man

> familiar us'd
> To sit indulgent, and with him partake
> Rural repast.

From the proximity of *familiar* (a proximity that is not only physical but also loving, as in a family), to the alienation of *distance* (God is in his Heaven, and all is not right with the world). From the innocence that shares a *rural repast*, to the guilt of tasting the fruit and its inevitable result, the *Distaste* of God.

[1] Lines 651, 732, 753, 777, 785, 863, 881, 929, 986, 988, 1017. The word is important to Milton because it links *knowledge* and the fruit, as in the Latin *sapere*.

But the full force of Milton's words is not released until we remember that the opening lines of Book IX reassert the opening of Book I, and that there are echoes in the phrasing. The first three lines of the poem receive a massively memorable emphasis:

> Of Mans First Disobedience, and the Fruit
> Of that Forbidden Tree, whose *mortal tast*
> Brought Death into *the World, and all our woe* . . .

The lines from Book IX run:

> On the part of Heav'n
> Now alienated, distance and *distaste*,
> Anger and just rebuke, and judgement giv'n,
> That brought into *this World a world of woe* . . .

The collocation is surely decisive. And to it could be added God's original command to Adam, where there is the same conjunction of 'taste' (stressed by *bitter*) and 'world of woe':

> shun to taste,
> And shun the bitter consequence: for know,
> The day thou eat'st thereof, my sole command
> Transgrest, inevitably thou shalt dye;
> From that day mortal, and this happie State
> Shalt loose, expell'd from hence into a World
> Of woe and sorrow. (VIII. 327–33)

'Distaste', then, is a richly triumphant pun, dignified because of its silence, bitter in the way it turns those notes to tragic. That the bitter dignity comes from the silence can be seen if we contrast the similar pun in Robert Armin's *Nest of Ninnies*: 'It is hard that the taste of one Apple should distaste the whole lumpe of this defused Chaios.'[1] *Distaste* there has none of the majesty of Milton's great rooted blossomer.

It is through the varying degrees of explicitness in word-play that Milton maintains the Grand Style, and also the necessary distinction between the epic itself and the characters in it. They are permitted to say things that would be

[1] 1608 (*Works*, ed. A. B. Grosart, 1880, p. 48).

indecorous for the epic writer in his own person. On this depends the success of *incarnate*, applied by Satan to himself in the snake (IX. 166). Bentley was shocked by the blasphemy, which Mr. Empson applauds as another imaginative parallel between Satan and Christ.[1] We find Empson in some slight measure anticipated by Hume: 'as *our blessed Saviour*'s taking our Nature upon him, is styled, *His Incarnation*'.[2] Yet above all it is the silence of the context which makes the word effective—any nudge from the poet would have been fatal to the Grand Style.

Likewise, when Eve has been led by the snake to the tree, her words contain two puns—one made by her, one by Milton: one explicit, one implicit.

> Serpent, we might have spar'd our coming hither,
> Fruitless to me, though Fruit be here to excess. (IX. 647–8)

The jaunty directness of *fruitless/fruit* would have been alien to the poet, but it is all too dramatically apt to Eve. Her levity at such a moment is tragic—which makes it rather misleading of Mr. Prince to describe the pun here as one of Milton's 'sports'.[3] Unlike Eve, Milton takes *fruit* too seriously, from the very first line of his epic, to be willing to sound brash about the fact that actions have consequences.[4] When in the closing lines of Book IX the poet wishes to show us the disappointed bitterness of Adam and Eve's awakening to guilt, he is careful to suppress one term of the pun:

> Thus they in mutual accusation spent
> The fruitless hours. (IX. 1187–8)

The pert vivacity of Eve has given way to the tragic notes of the poet.

'Fruitless to me, though Fruit be here *to excess*': that pun is made by Milton. Eve means no more than to be wittily disgruntled. Milton reminds us, again in ominous silence,

[1] *Some Versions*, p. 165. [2] p. 249.

[3] *The Italian Element*, p. 124.

[4] On Milton's *fruit* and *knowledge* see Cleanth Brooks, 'Milton and Critical Re-estimates', *P.M.L.A.*, 1951.

that she speaks more truly than she realizes, that there is indeed fruit 'to excess'. It will not be long before we see Adam and Eve 'bewailing thir excess' (XI. 111). And it will be clear that the pun in *to excess* is unspoken rather than non-existent, if one remembers the particular application of 'excess' to 'intemperance in eating or drinking' (*O.E.D.* 5b), and so its traditional aptness to Adam and Eve:

> Adam oure fader, and his wyf also,
> Fro Paradys to labour and to wo
> Were dryven for that vice, it is no drede.
> For whil that Adam fasted, as I rede,
> He was in Paradys; and whan that he
> Eet of the fruyt deffended on the tree,
> Anon he was out cast to wo and peyne.
> O glotonye, on thee wel oghte us pleyne!
> O, wiste a man how manye maladyes
> Folwen of excesse and of glotonyes . . .
>
> (*The Pardoner's Tale*)

Sombre and quiet equivocation is characteristic of Milton. Richardson noticed that when Eve tries to persuade Adam, her language makes clear how much is really at stake:

> Were it I thought Death menac't would ensue
> This my attempt, I would sustain alone
> The worst, and not perswade thee, rather die
> Deserted, then oblige thee with a fact
> Pernicious to thy Peace. (IX. 977–81)

'Fact' has its common sense of crime,[1] and with 'Death . . . die . . . pernicious', it hardens *oblige* into a death-sentence: 'the Word *Oblige* here', said Richardson, 'is capable of a Double Sense. Either to Tie to, to Drag Along With, or After, or to make Guilty, and Punishable, to Devote to Death . . . Both Senses are Included.'[2] The harder sense insists on the tragedy; the milder sense allows Eve (even at the moment in which she makes her tragic gesture) to suggest that perhaps things will not be so bad after all. Such a use of

[1] *O.E.D.* 1c. 'in the 16th and 17th centuries the commonest sense'.

[2] p. 432.

language, whether as a form of metaphor or of word-play, triumphantly observes decorum without fixing its virtue as in a frost.

VII. POSTSCRIPT

There is always the danger in discussing Milton's Grand Style of assuming that it is merely grand, of conceding too much, of leaning over backwards not to make claims. Professor Kenneth Muir, for instance, is unnecessarily magnanimous on Milton's behalf when he says that 'it is futile to expect the nervous energy, the subtle involutions of style, the tentacular imagery, the linguistic daring and the colloquial ease of Shakespeare's best verse'.[1] This is true, if it means no more than that Shakespeare's best verse is better than anybody else's. But beyond that—no, Milton's style *does* command nervous energy, subtle involutions, tentacular imagery, and linguistic daring—though these often take unShakespearian forms. (Colloquial ease we may dispense with, as an extraordinary critical shibboleth.)

Yet Milton's grandeur and his subtlety (my concern in the next chapter) often co-exist in the very same lines, which makes it particularly important not to cordon off the poem from meddling practical critics. The following lines would generally be agreed to belong to Milton's sterner style, but their bareness is combined with local subtlety to produce an effect of astonishing breadth and power:

> So glister'd the dire Snake, and into fraud
> Led Eve our credulous Mother, to the Tree
> Of prohibition, root of all our woe. (IX. 643–5)

These lines stamp themselves at once as in the Grand Style. What is remarkable, though, is that they are verbally subtle and active without any fussiness or any blurring of the grand austerity. I am thinking not only of the sombre gleam in the pun on *root*; but also of subtler effects: the playing of the bright *glister'd* against the dark *dire*, for instance. Or the

[1] *John Milton* (1955; 2nd ed., 1960), pp. 134–5.

superb use of the curt 'snake'. (Milton calls it the serpent fifteen times in Book IX; but the snake only three times: once literally, before Satan enters it; and twice with calculated brutality: 'So talk'd the spirited sly Snake', and here.)

There is the superbly suggestive diction: 'our credulous Mother', which must be one of the finest, most delicate, and most moving of all the oxymorons in the poem. A mother ought to be everything that is reliable and wise—here she is credulous. And *our* clinches the effect; *credulous* is pinioned on each side ('our . . . Mother'), and the full tragic pathos of the oxymoron is released. Sylvester's Du Bartas has two unusually good lines using 'credulous', but in the end how much smaller they are:

> poor Woman, wavering, weak, unwise,
> Light, credulous, news-lover, giv'n to lies.[1]

There is the majesty of 'the Tree of prohibition'—no mere stilted Latinism, since it is literally true: the Tree is not just 'the prohibited Tree', but the Tree of *all* prohibition. And there is at this fatal moment the ringing echo of the opening lines of the poem in 'all our woe'. But perhaps the most irresistible of all the effects here is syntactical. 'Into fraud led Eve . . .' overlaps magnificently with '. . . led Eve to the Tree', so that what begins as a moving and ancient moral metaphor (lead us not into temptation) crystallizes with terrifying literalness. There is a touching change of focus, superbly compressed and yet without a shock or a jerk.

But the astonishing thing is not that these excellent explicable subtleties are there, but that they do not at all disturb the lines' serene, almost Dantesque, austerity. Milton, as so often, combines what are apparently incompatible greatnesses. Hazlitt remarked that 'the fervour of his imagination melts down and renders malleable, as in a furnace, the most contradictory materials'.[2]

[1] Sylvester's *Works*, ed. Grosart, i. 109.

[2] *Works*, ed. Howe, v. 58.

Clearly even those passages which are most in the Grand Style may also contain riches of a different kind. Macaulay[1] was right to insist on how many and varied are the excellences of Milton's style, 'that style, which no rival has been able to equal, and no parodist to degrade, which displays in their highest perfection the idiomatic powers of the English tongue, and to which every ancient and every modern language has contributed something of grace, of energy, or of music'.

[1] 'Milton' (1825). *Literary and Historical Essays* (1934), p. 9.

3. Enhancing Suggestions

For Bagehot, *Paradise Lost* was distinguished not only by 'a manly strength', but also by its 'haunting atmosphere of enhancing suggestions'.[1] And these suggestions are not just a matter of the great vistas of Milton's themes, but also of delicate and subtle life in the verse. This chapter tries to show how Milton, without abandoning epic grandeur, draws on the infinite suggestiveness of word-order and words.

The eighteenth-century critics were quick to spot these effects. So Addison, talking of such rhetorical patterning, says that 'several passages in Milton . . . have as excellent turns of this nature as any of our English poets whatsoever; but [I] shall only mention that which follows, in which he describes the fallen angels engaged in the intricate disputes of predestination, free-will, and foreknowledge; and to humour the perplexity, makes a kind of labyrinth in the very words that describe it':[2]

> reason'd high
> Of Providence, Foreknowledge, Will, and Fate,
> Fixt Fate, free will, foreknowledge absolute,
> And found no end, in wandring mazes lost. (II. 558–61)

Similarly Richardson commented on the lines in which Satan looks into Chaos before leaping into it: ' 'tis Observable the

[1] 1859. *Literary Studies* (1905), ii. 217.

[2] *The Tatler*, No. 114, 31 Dec. 1709. Cp. William Smith: 'the very Structure of the Words expresses the Intricacy of the Discourse; and the Repetition of some of the Words, with Epithets of slow Pronunciation, shews the Difficulty of making Advancements, in such unfathomable Points' (*Longinus on the Sublime*, 2nd ed., 1742, p. 185).

Poet Himself seems to be Doing what he Describes, for the Period begins at 910. Then he goes not On Directly, but Lingers; giving an Idea of *Chaos* before he Enters into it':[1]

> Into this wilde Abyss,
> The Womb of nature and perhaps her Grave,
> Of neither Sea, nor Shore, nor Air, nor Fire,
> But all these in thir pregnant causes mixt
> Confus'dly, and which thus must ever fight,
> Unless th' Almighty Maker them ordain
> His dark materials to create more Worlds,
> Into this wild Abyss the warie fiend
> Stood on the brink of Hell and look'd a while,
> Pondering his Voyage . . . (II. 910–19)

In the same spirit, Newton too noticed how 'the Poet Himself seems to be Doing what he Describes' in praising the lines

> Thir song was partial, but the harmony
> (What could it less when Spirits immortal sing?)
> Suspended Hell, and took with ravishment
> The thronging audience. (II. 552–5)

'*The harmony suspended Hell*; but is it not much better with the parenthesis coming between? which suspends as it were the event, raises the reader's attention, and gives a greater force to the sentence.'[2] What makes the sentence delicate as well as forceful is the way the syntactical effect echoes the play on *suspend*—suspension as a technical harmonic term.

Newton also quoted an excellent comment by William Benson:

> Thus at thir shadie Lodge arriv'd, both stood,
> Both turnd, and under op'n Skie ador'd
> The God . . . (IV. 720–2)

'This artful Manner of writing makes the Reader see them *Stop* and *Turn* to worship God before they went into their Bower. If this Manner was alter'd, much of the Effect of the Painting would be lost.

[1] p. 81. [2] i. 118.

And now arriving at their shady Lodge
Both stopt, *both turn'd*, and under open Sky
Ador'd the God, *&c.*'[1]

Plainly there will always be differences of opinion about such effects, but Benson does seem to be pointing to a genuine function of the line-ending: the verse wheels, just as Adam and Eve wheel.

Presumably it was rhetorical training as well as confidence in Milton's exactitude which made the eighteenth-century critics take his syntax seriously. They assumed that it meant what it said, even if this sometimes necessitated supposing that he was a subtle poet. So Richardson drew attention to Eve's leaving Adam:

Thus saying, from her Husbands hand her hand
Soft she withdrew . . . (IX. 385–6)

' 'Tis Pity any Reader should Overlook the Beauty and Force of This Passage. Impatient to Compleat her Conquest, while she was yet speaking what did not really Convince Herself, she was Going; His Forc'd Consent is finely Mark'd, she Drew away Her Hand from His, yet Wishing to Detain her, Loath, Dreading to Part. In vain! 'tis a Master-Touch of Tenderness in Few Words.'[2] And Richardson is as sensitive in his comment on the syntax when Eve

as oft engag'd
To be returnd by Noon amid the Bowre. (IX. 400–1)

'*Return'd*, as if Already done; very Elegant and New, and full of Energy.'[3]

Such syntactical mirroring is of a rather obvious kind, as were most of the instances pointed out in the eighteenth century. But it provides solid reason for thinking that Milton had a real interest in expressive syntax, and so it justifies an investigation into subtler effects. Sometimes such subtlety closely resembles that of eighteenth-century poetry. When

[1] *Letters Concerning Poetical Translations* (1739), p. 48.
[2] p. 410.
[3] p. 412 (misnumbered 421).

Pope tells us that Atticus manages to 'Just hint a fault, and hesitate dislike', his adaptation of *hesitate* to a transitive instead of an intransitive verb carries a weight of condemnation: other people just hesitate, Atticus's hesitation is active, a tool that he uses.[1] So in Milton a lowring sky does not merely scowl—it scowls snow:

> the lowring Element
> Scowls ore the dark'nd lantskip Snow, or showre. (II. 490–1)

I. LIQUID TEXTURE

The eighteenth-century editors were well aware of, though often exasperated by, the fluidity of Milton's syntax—the hesitations as to which are main verbs, the clustering of dependent clauses, and the indivisible or variously divisible flow. Pearce enjoyed 'for the sake of Perspicuity inserting the Note of a Parenthesis'.[2] Mr. Empson dryly observes that at one point Bentley 'let in a couple of main verbs, like ferrets'.[3]

But in the eighteenth century they were also clear about the advantages of such a style: its combination of a wide suggestiveness with the momentum of statement. So Richardson commented on the lines describing Adam's first view of Paradise:

> all things smil'd,
> With fragrance and with joy my heart oreflow'd. (VIII. 265–6)

Richardson saw that it would make a difference to move the comma to after *fragrance*: 'The Difference is only in the Placing of a Comma, but That Vary's the Sence considerably. In the One *Adam* says, All things Smiling, his Heart overflow'd with Fragrance and Joy; in the Other, that All things Smil'd with Fragrance, and his Heart o'erflow'd with Joy: Both are Beautyful . . . but This Sense [the former] is

[1] *O.E.D.* 3. '*trans.* To express or say with hesitation'—the first example is Pope.

[2] p. 58; also pp. 35, 92, 99. And Matthias Mull, a bizarre latter-day Bentley (1884), has three pages listing necessary parentheses.

[3] *Some Versions*, p. 160.

the Best; it takes in the other, and with an Additional, and more Noble Idea. All things Smile, not with Fragrance Only, but in Every respect. That Universal Balmy, Cordial, Exhilarating Air which He breath'd continually whilst he Beheld the General Lovelyness around him is also Express'd, together with the Overflowing Joy Arising from All.'[1]

That is excellently said, and finely brings out the merits of the flowing syntax, its terminations no more than hints:

> So evenings die, in their green going,
> A wave, interminably flowing.

Milton's line and a half can be divided in many ways, the sense varying minutely each time:

1. All things smil'd,
   With fragrance and with joy my heart oreflow'd.
2. All things smil'd with fragrance,
   And with joy my heart oreflow'd.
3. All things smil'd with fragrance and with joy,
   My heart oreflow'd.
4. All things smil'd,
   With fragrance and with joy,
   My heart oreflow'd.

In the last case, the fragrance and the joy would fit Pearce's description of a phrase elsewhere in Milton, 'so plac'd between the two Sentences as equally to relate to both'.[2] The fragrance and the joy would be poised between both Nature and Adam, just as Adam himself is poised: fragrance without, and joy within. Not that we need to break the verse down like this in reading—its flow keeps us moving. But to do so is instructive, and confirms Richardson's understanding of the syntax. And the word 'oreflow'd' alerts us to the function of the syntax, itself overflowing. Everything smiles, is fragrant, is joyful, overflows; the harmony of Eden, in itself and between man and nature, is once again beautifully captured.

[1] p. 367.

[2] pp. 154–5. See p. 86 below. Also the comment on 'grateful to Heaven', p. 114 below.

The overflowing is itself a tribute to the Creator. Comus perverted the truthful tribute, and tried (like Satan) 'out of good still to find means of evil'; but Rilke restored the truth in speaking to God:

> Thus every superabundance flows to you.
> And as a fountain's upper basin stands
> for ever overstreaming, as with strands
> of loosened hair, into the lowest bowl,
> into your valleys will their fullness roll
> whenever things and thoughts are overflowing.[1]

Nor is this an isolated syntactical effect. Milton's first commentator drew attention to it in his note on 'transported I behold, transported touch' (VIII. 529–30): 'Pleas'd to excess, I find my Feeling pleasant to excess: Raised above my self, I perceive my Feeling raised as far above it self: Or carried beyond my self I perceive my sense of Touching carried too beyond what's usual.'[2]

After the Fall, Adam cries out to the trees to shelter him from seeing God and his angels. It is a very simple cry:

> Cover me ye Pines,
> Ye Cedars, with innumerable boughs
> Hide me . . . (IX. 1088–90)

The cry is not made less simple if one points out that here too the syntax is curiously fluid, that one may divide it at all sorts of places:

1. Cover me ye Pines,
   Ye Cedars, with innumerable boughs hide me.
2. Cover me
   Ye Pines, ye Cedars,
   With innumerable boughs hide me.
3. Cover me ye Pines, ye Cedars,
   With innumerable boughs hide me.
4. Cover me ye Pines, ye Cedars, with innumerable boughs
   Hide me.

[1] *The Book of Hours*, tr. J. B. Leishman.

[2] Hume, p. 239.

All these cries are equally simple, but all are slightly different. The punctuation selects from among them, of course, just as it did in the other examples. But the effect of the two lines is as of innumerable cries, as of innumerable boughs, to innumerable trees—all of which telescope into one terrifyingly simple cry. And just as 'oreflow'd' was a signal in Richardson's example, so here is 'innumerable'.

Perhaps such a comment on the syntax may seem less far-fetched if we notice how it is analogous to the patterns of rhyme which Mr. Prince has traced in *Lycidas*, 'a type of rhyme which looks both back and forward'.[1]

The effect is similar to that which Hopkins gains in the phrase 'My lament is cries countless', where he brilliantly uses what always seems the mysterious construction of single subject, single verb, plural complement. One lament, countless cries; and the 'is' acts as a funnel from which they pour. Milton, the poet who wrote with splendid liberty that 'Both Death and I am found eternal' (tersely thrusting home the single nature of death and Adam)—Milton is in many ways not so different a poet from Hopkins as some believe.

Taking his cue from the eighteenth century, Mr. Empson brought out more fully what Milton gained. Bentley had disapproved of the phrase 'words or tongue':

> to recount Almightie works
> What words or tongue of Seraph can suffice,
> Or heart of man suffice to comprehend? (VII. 112–14)

Bentley's emendation to *words from tongue*, as Mr. Empson says, 'loses the completeness of the statement; "How can any stage in the production of the speech of seraphs be adequate; how can they find words, and if they could how could their tongues pronounce them?" But besides this, the merit of *or* is its fluidity; the way it allows "words from tongue" to be suggested without pausing for analysis, without holding up the single movement of the line.'[2]

[1] *The Italian Element*, p. 86.
[2] *Some Versions*, p. 161.

If we want 'the completeness of the statement' in words other than Milton's (and, in particular, in different syntax), expressing it is a lengthy matter. See, for instance, the censorious attempts to rephrase that magnificent compression, 'Yet Virgin of Proserpina from Jove'. And one can support Mr. Empson's comment on 'words or tongue' by referring to another use of *or*, where Milton, as often, shows the classical virtue of being original with the minimum of alteration. Satan laments among the beauties of Paradise:

> I in none of these
> Find place or refuge. (IX. 118–19)

Bentley[1] wanted to alter this to 'place of refuge', but just as 'words or tongue' suggested 'words from tongue' while making a more complete statement, so here does 'place or refuge' suggest 'place of refuge'—while also saying something stronger: Satan not only cannot find 'place of refuge', he cannot find *place* in Paradise. Newton provided the paraphrase '*I in none of these find place* to dwell in *or refuge* from divine vengeance. And this sense seems to be confirm'd by what follows. "But neither here seek I, no nor in Heaven / *To dwell*". '[2] The 'Heaven on Earth' offers no more place to Satan than does Heaven itself. That is no country for Satan —the young 'imparadis't in one anothers arms', birds in the trees. . . .

Mr. Empson adds a valuable insight into the reason for Milton's fluid syntax: 'Milton aims both at a compact and weighty style, which requires short clauses, and a sustained style with the weight of momentum, which requires long clauses.'[3] Furthermore, another of his examples shows that Milton can use the fluidity of his syntax both for an immediately dramatic reason and also to establish an important link. In Eve's dream, the false angel tempts her to be

> not to Earth confind,
> But somtimes in the Air, as wee, somtimes
> Ascend to Heav'n. (V. 78–80)

[1] p. 270. [2] ii. 132. [3] *Some Versions*, p. 161.

'The Words *as we*', remarked Pearce, 'are so plac'd between the two Sentences as equally to relate to both, and in the first Sentence the Verb *be* is understood. Dr. Bentley has alter'd this Passage thus, "*But sometimes* RANGE *in Air*, *sometimes*, *as we*, *&c.*" But in this reading of the Doctor's are not the Angels excluded from ranging in the Air?'[1]

Mr. Empson adds with characteristic subtlety, and with characteristic respect for Milton's subtlety, 'Surely there is a dramatic reason for the gawkiness of the line here; the doubt implied as to whether he could go to Heaven himself shows a natural embarrassment in the disguised Satan.'[2] But the more important point—and it is stressed in *Milton's God*[3] —is that the syntax throws heavy stress on the words 'as wee'. We can't help noticing them, they hook themselves on to our memory, and it is they as much as the other diction which make manifest the grim coincidence later in the same Book when Raphael tells Adam and Eve that they may, because of what they eat,

> wingd ascend
> Ethereal, as wee, or may at choice
> Here or in Heav'nly Paradises dwell. (v. 498–500)

Eve perversely misunderstands that 'choice', and it is a detail of syntax that helps to make the point.

Mr. C. S. Lewis is not on the whole sympathetic to Mr. Empson's kind of criticism, but he too adds some excellent amplifications of the eighteenth-century view of Milton's syntax. Let me quote one of the best pieces of stylistic comment in *A Preface to Paradise Lost* (it is a great pity that there are not more pages about the style): 'A fixed order of words is the price—an all but ruinous price—which English pays for being uninflected. The Miltonic constructions enable the poet to depart, in some degree, from this fixed order and thus to drop the ideas into his sentence in any order he chooses. Thus, for example,

[1] pp. 154–5. [2] *Some Versions*, p. 163. [3] p. 150.

> soft oppression seis'd
> My droused sense, untroubl'd, though I thought
> I then was passing to my former state
> Insensible, and forthwith to dissolve. (VIII, 291)

The syntax is so artificial that it is ambiguous. I do not know whether *untroubled* qualifies *me* understood, or *sense*, and similar doubts arise about *insensible* and the construction of *to dissolve*. But then I don't need to know. The sequence *drowsed—untroubled—my former state—insensible—dissolve* is exactly right; the very crumbling of consciousness is before us and the fringe of syntactical mystery helps rather than hinders the effect.'[1]

That is an excellent point, even though the wording of it is at times rather bluffly casual. 'Any order he chooses' sounds a bit light-hearted or wilful for the sort of choice to which a great poet is impelled; and 'I don't need to know' sounds almost like relief or Terror of the Cognitive, and would be liable to invite a sharp riposte from the anti-Miltonists. Nevertheless, they would be wrong, and Mr. Lewis is right.

II. TINCTURE OR REFLECTION

Milton's magnificent lines on the creation of Light are a noble comment on his own poetry and its light:

> Of Light by farr the greater part he took,
> Transplanted from her cloudie Shrine, and plac'd
> In the Suns Orb, made porous to receive
> And drink the liquid Light, firm to retaine
> Her gather'd beams, great Palace now of Light.
> Hither as to thir Fountain other Starrs
> Repairing, in thir gold'n Urns draw Light,
> And hence the Morning Planet guilds his horns;
> By tincture or reflection they augment
> Thir small peculiar, though from human sight
> So farr remote, with diminution seen . . . (VII. 359–69)

By far the greater part of the light of Milton's poetry acts with the noble directness of the sun itself. The Grand Style

[1] pp. 45–46.

is a 'great Palace now of Light'. That directness ensures that we receive the rays of the sun—the sun which is like poetry in that its

> vertue on it self works no effect,
> But in the fruitful Earth; there first receavd
> His beams, unactive else, thir vigor find. (VIII. 95–97)

But not all the radiance of Milton's poetry is shed in this way. Like the light, it too is liquid; and it too is both porous and firm. And just as the stars receive and transmit light by 'tincture or reflection', so too do Milton's words. If we are to see not merely the greater part of the light, but all of it, we must receive the tinctures and reflections which gild his liquid verse.

Richardson offers a good example of what I mean. He drew attention to the suggestiveness of the placing of 'retir'd' in the lines

> Others apart sat on a Hill retir'd,
> In thoughts more elevate, and reason'd high . . . (II. 557–8)

'Though the Text does not Say it, the Reader will from the Words naturally be led to imagine Some were Retir'd, in Thought, as well as from the Company, and Reason'd and Debated, Discours'd within Themselves, on these Perplexing, but Important Suttleties: This gives a very Proper Image here, a very Melancholly and Touching One.'[1] Richardson's tone, tentative yet precise, is admirable—and so is his insistence that many of Milton's images depend on what is suggested as well as on what is explicitly said. The modern critic is often accused of reading too much into works of the past, and certainly he ought to point precisely to what it is that suggested his comments. But it is interesting to find the eighteenth-century critics responding to Milton in so supple a way.

An interchange between Bentley and Pearce brings out that flexible syntax in Milton can be mistaken for careless syntax. Bentley objected to the description of Satan,

[1] p. 63.

His count'nance, as the Morning Starr that guides
The starrie flock, allur'd them, and with lyes
Drew after him the third part of Heav'ns Host. (v. 705–7)

'In this Reading the Construction will be, *His countenance allured and drew them with Lies*. He is the *Father of Lies* indeed, if not his Tongue, but his Countenance spoke them.'[1] Of course this is a quibble—such a shift is easy enough, and the main meaning offers no real difficulty. But as often with a quibble by Bentley, he fastens on a boldly suggestive metaphor: 'He is the *Father of Lies* indeed, if not his Tongue, but his Countenance spoke them.' And Pearce's reply brings out very well both the straightforward sense and the metaphorical suggestion: 'By the expression *His Countenance* is meant He himself. . . . But if this will not be allow'd to be *Milton*'s meaning, yet it may be said that *Satan's Countenance* seducing his followers by disguising the foul intentions of his heart, may be very properly said to *seduce with Lyes*.'[2] That Pearce's suggestion is plausible may be seen from the innumerable occasions when Milton makes profound and subtle use of Satan's countenance.

At any rate, the fact that the solid and respectable eighteenth-century editors were aware of suggestive niceties of syntax gives one some right to proceed.

After long argument, Eve leaves Adam to go gardening on her own:

Thus saying, from her Husbands hand her hand
Soft she withdrew. (IX. 385–6)

If we had to paraphrase the lines, we would say that 'soft' was an adverb, not an adjective: she softly withdrew her hand. This makes admirably grim sense; *soft* ought to include 'yielding', but Eve is firmly and unshakeably insisting on her own way. She is stubborn but sweet:

Eve, who thought
Less attributed to her Faith sincere,
Thus her reply with accent sweet renewd. (IX. 319–21)

[1] p. 172. [2] p. 185.

Persistent, but meek:

> but Eve
> Persisted, yet submiss, though last, repli'd. (IX. 376–7)

And she is obdurate but soft. So much for the main sense: she softly withdrew her hand. But Milton didn't exactly say that; and since 'soft' is the adjectival form as well, and since Milton so often puts his adjectives after his nouns, the word 'soft' gets attracted into Eve's hand, delicately and as it were by reflection. So that the total effect is 'her soft hand softly she withdrew', with *soft* sounded much more quietly than *softly*. And with a delicate fusion of two points of view, since the adverb has the neutrality of an onlooker, while the adjective puts us in the place of Adam as he feels Eve's hand. E. E. Cummings might achieve such effects through typography and punctuation—Milton uses syntax. Mr. Lewis's remark about Milton's network is applicable to his syntax too: 'Nearly every sentence in Milton has that power which physicists sometimes think we shall have to attribute to matter—the power of action at a distance.'[1]

This is obviously open to the charge of over-ingenuity, and substantiation is scarce. (It would be likely to be, with so delicate an effect.) But, first, one might point to softness as pre-eminently the characteristic for which Eve was created:

> For contemplation hee and valour formd,
> For softness shee and sweet attractive Grace. (IV. 297–8)

Her 'soft imbraces' and 'her Heav'nly forme Angelic, but more soft, and Feminine' are contrasted elsewhere with Adam, 'Less winning soft, less amiablie milde'.[2]

And, second, one might support this with the lines when Adam awakens Eve, which interestingly give us the 'hand' again:

[1] *A Preface*, p. 42. J. H. Hanford has two particularly interesting pages on the beauty of Milton's ambiguous syntax in *A Milton Handbook* (4th ed., 1946, pp. 300–1). And John Wain, discussing Hopkins, has deftly pointed out the suggestiveness of a verb 'that radiates both ways' (*Proceedings of the British Academy*, 1959, xlv. 194).

[2] IV. 471; IX. 457–8; IV. 479.

> then with voice
> Milde, as when Zephyrus on Flora breathes,
> Her hand soft touching, whisperd thus . . . (v. 15–17)

In the eighteenth century this was seen to be ambiguous, and was tidied up with a hyphen: *soft-touching*. And again if we had to choose, the paraphrase would obviously be 'softly touching'. But the close parallel with the other line reinforces for me the idea that 'soft' once again affects our sense of Eve's hand, a tincture that is quietly beautiful, and that would certainly deserve Bagehot's praise of Milton's 'haunting atmosphere of enhancing suggestions'.

To combine clarity of stated sense with such suggestiveness is the mark of those poets who rise above divisions into Classical and Romantic. Milton's use of syntax for such purposes is often supported by alliteration, which—like rhyme—can tie together suggestively things which are not tied together in the plain statement. This was perhaps one of the many effects which Hopkins developed from Milton. Take, for instance, the alliteration in the line from 'I wake and feel the fell of dark, not day', when Hopkins says that the heart must endure more before it reaches God's peace: 'And more must, in yet longer light's delay.' Obviously a simple paraphrase would say 'While light delays even longer', but that is not what Hopkins wrote. The compression of the syntax, itself Miltonic, brings *longer* up against *light*, which furthermore alliterates. And the alliteration is stressed by the opening of the line ('and more must . . .'). So that although logically, and primarily, *longer* goes with *delay*, and not with *light*, the effect of the syntax and alliteration is to suggest that it is light which is longer. So that it is as if, thinking apparently only of the fact that it will be a long time before God's peace comes, Hopkins also remembers that when the light of eternity does come, it will be *longer* than the darkness of this life. The phrase has just that combination of strong present despair and quiet distant hope which is characteristic of his best poetry.

Milton uses syntax and alliteration in just the same way—

they allow him to suggest things which he doesn't actually say. In the account of Mulciber's fall, for example, we move through 'he fell . . . he fell . . . dropt' to

> He with this rebellious rout
> Fell long before; nor aught avail'd him now
> To have built in Heav'n high Towrs; nor did he scape
> By all his Engins, but was headlong sent . . . (I. 747–50)

Alliteration and word-order tie 'Heav'n' and 'high' together, though the plain sense is 'high Towrs', enforced as it is by the rhythm as well as by the earlier reference to 'a Towred structure high'. But Milton is not satisfied with the plain sense alone. The feeling of *high Heav'n* is important to the sense of Mulciber's fall from that height, Mulciber who fell headlong down to Hell. To say that Heaven is high would be to risk cliché; but to suggest it while saying something else is another matter.

The support for this comes in the way Milton uses 'high' elsewhere. It is used more than a hundred times; and he uses it in the immediate context of 'Heaven' more than twenty times, without actually applying it, with dull predictability, to 'Heaven'. Only twice does he say that Heaven is high—but the one is tinged with a moral meaning, stressed by 'lowly':

> Heav'n is for thee too high
> To know what passes there; be lowlie wise. (VIII. 172–3)

And the other is Eve's silly hopefulness:

> Heav'n is high,
> High and remote to see from thence distinct
> Each thing on Earth. (IX. 811–13)

But most worth noticing is that Milton is very fond of using this same pattern elsewhere to bring 'Heaven' and 'high' together while stating something else: 'Heav'ns high jurisdiction', or 'Heav'ns high behest'.[1] Perhaps the closest to the pattern of 'in Heav'n high Towrs' is this sequence:

[1] This is the pattern at II. 62, 319, 359; V. 220, 467; VII. 373; XI. 251.

> Had not th' Eternal King Omnipotent
> From his strong hold of Heav'n high over-rul'd
> And limited thir might. (VI. 227–9)

'High' there is an adverb, but how finely the syntax and alliteration merge it with 'Heav'n'. (Or conversely, if it is taken as an adjective, how finely it suggests the moral power of the adverb.)

Yet one can bring out the point of such a merging only by leaving syntax for a moment in order to stress the crucial importance to Milton of the word 'high', partly reflected in its great frequency. Just as 'stand' is clashed against 'fall', so is 'high' clashed against 'deep': 'the deep fall of those too high aspiring' (VI. 898–9).[1] Insisting on 'the highth of this great Argument', a height that must be worthy of Him who sits 'High Thron'd above all highth', Milton simply but powerfully plays the literal against the abstract:

> nor ever thence
> Had ris'n or heav'd his head, but that the will
> And high permission of all-ruling Heaven . . . (I. 210–12)

The play is in earnest because the physical fact about Heaven has a moral significance:

> Strait knew him all the Bands
> Of Angels under watch; and to his state,
> And to his message high in honour rise. (V. 287–9)

And Milton even makes the word receive the full weight of his sardonic condemnation. Pandaemonium, 'the high Capital of Satan and his Peers', is down in Hell. There 'highly they rag'd against the Highest'. And there we hear of Dagon, who 'fell flat, and sham'd his Worshipers', and yet 'had his Temple high'.[2]

Milton uses such fluidity of syntax so that it both makes clear sense and also is suggestive. Sometimes the suggestion is of a hyperbolical beauty which it would be indecorous to

[1] Mrs. I. G. MacCaffrey writes interestingly on this in chapters iii and iv of *P.L. as 'Myth'*. Jackson I. Cope goes through all the examples in chapter iv of *The Metaphoric Structure of P.L.* (1962).

[2] I. 756, 666, 461–3.

state as fact—particularly in the epic. To show this at work, it is best to take one of the most powerful and consistent of the Paradisal images: the mingled beauties of sight and of scent (and of sound too). The image itself is a lovely one, but it is the mingling syntax which brings it to life, which both suggests the magically pre-lapsarian and states the matter of fact. The syntax combines the charmed subjectivity of the lyric with the grave objectivity of the epic. Macaulay thought that poetry and science were the ends of a see-saw: 'We cannot unite the incompatible advantages of reality and deception, the clear discernment of truth and the exquisite enjoyment of fiction.'[1] Milton often did, as Richardson insisted: 'When the Imagination is Rais'd as much as Possible, let it still know More is Un-conceiv'd; Let the Lark Sing after he is Lost in Air.'[2]

When we see Eve as she

> strews the ground
> With Rose and Odours from the shrub unfum'd, (v. 348–9)

we know perfectly well what is meant and find no unseemly violence of syntax. But the actual sequence—'strews the ground with odours'—makes the scents magically visible and physical. So, too, does the superb word-order in these lines:

> So to the Silvan Lodge
> They came, that like Pomona's Arbour smil'd
> With flourets deck't and fragrant smells; but Eve
> Undeckt . . . (v. 377–80)

If we want simple sense, then 'deck't' goes only with 'flourets' and not with 'smells'—'deck't with smells' might be too boldly metaphorical if baldly stated. But the lines do obliquely state it, and the encircling of 'fragrant smells' by *deck't* and *undeckt* ensures that the metaphor is not so obliquely presented as to be itself invisible. The imagination once again treats scents as if they were as solid and visible as flowers. And there is also a perfectly intelligible non-meta-

[1] *Literary and Historical Essays* (1934), pp. 7–8.

[2] p. 41.

phorical syntax ('smil'd with fragrant smells and deck't with flourets'). The lines combine the virtues of both poetry and prose. Moreover, they achieve through syntax the mingling of the senses which Keats achieves through diction: 'Nor what soft incense hangs upon the boughs.'

This particular image for the beauty of Paradise can take simpler forms. There is the syntactical stroke of describing 'Cassia, Nard, and Balme' not—as we would expect—as 'odorous flowers', but as 'flouring Odours'. Bentley found the phrase 'Affectation extravagant';[1] Pearce paltered;[2] and it was left to Richardson to maintain that the phrase was a fine one.[3] And the beautifully unexpected substantiality of the scents here is skilfully introduced by 'field' and 'Groves':

> and now is come
> Into the blissful field, through Groves of Myrrhe,
> And flouring Odours, Cassia, Nard, and Balme. (v. 291–3)

Or the syntactical imagination can juxtapose 'Rose' and 'Odours' as if they were of equal substantiality, and then apply to them both a verb that, in its vigour, insists on the substantial:

> fresh Gales and gentle Aires
> Whisper'd it to the Woods, and from thir wings
> Flung Rose, flung Odours from the spicie Shrub. (VIII. 515–17)

The close parallel there with the first passage quoted above (v. 348–9) brings out how important to Milton is this image of Paradise. (The biographical critic would justifiably make at once for Milton's blindness.) And the poet invests Eve with this image as Satan fatally finds her:

> Eve separate he spies,
> Veil'd in a Cloud of Fragrance, where she stood,
> Half spi'd . . . (IX. 424–6)

The veil and the cloud make the roses' scent beautifully visible—does 'Half spi'd' even perhaps suggest that the scent was so thick that it almost hid her? Not really, because I have cut short the sentence:

[1] p. 157. [2] p. 169. [3] p. 218.

Half spi'd, so thick the Roses bushing round
About her glowd.

Reasonably, it is not the scent but the roses which hide her. But the other instances of Milton's seeing a scent, and the general fluidity of his syntax, persuade me that we are meant for a moment to believe that 'Half spi'd' follows the *Fragrance*, just as it follows 'he spies'. Of course it in fact anticipates the roses, but the deliberate 'flicker of hesitation' which Dr. Davie[1] finds elsewhere in Milton is perhaps being used here with characteristic subtlety. Like a skilful advocate, Milton says something which would be impermissibly far-fetched, and then has it struck from the record. But his skill has lodged it in our minds or feelings.

Obviously such a device, to offer and then to deny (which has much in common with the rhetorical figure *occupatio*) is very common in Milton, above all in the allusions but also in the syntax. Bentley objected to the line 'The fellows of his crime, the followers rather': 'This RATHER, this correction of what he had said before, has something little and low in it. For if the Word wanted correcting, why was it put down here.'[2] But Bentley ought to allow that unsaying is not the same as never having said—and Milton makes fine use of the difference. It is on this that the poignant aptness of the classical allusions depends: Mulciber fell, but no—'Thus they relate, erring.'

The 'flicker of hesitation' which Dr. Davie so well defined, and which he so well illustrated in its effects, is not as uncommon in Milton as might be suggested by Dr. Davie's deploring of the average run of the syntax. Milton uses the slightly surprising compression of a double syntax to carry the weightiest suggestions. The syntax is not usually double in that it actually takes two paths—that would defeat narrative and sequence. But it stands for a moment uncertain which of two paths to take, and deliberately exploiting the uncertainty. Later, when we look back, we feel not only the

[1] See p. 42 above. [2] p. 27.

relief of having chosen, but also a powerful sense of what the other path led to.

> Footfalls echo in the memory
> Down the passage which we did not take
> Towards the door we never opened
> Into the rose-garden. My words echo
> Thus, in your mind.

Milton can combine, through the hesitations of his syntax, the suggestiveness of vistas with the progressions of ordered narrative.

This is so when Adam tragically exclaims

> O much deceav'd, much failing, hapless Eve,
> Of thy presum'd return! event perverse!
> Thou never from that houre in Paradise
> Foundst either sweet repast, or sound repose . . . (IX. 404–7)

At first, one takes 'deceav'd' and 'failing' as absolute in their application to Eve—the poet's imagination is absorbing the full bitterness of the imminent Fall. But then the next line—'Of thy presum'd return!'—declares that she is *deceived in* the one present circumstance: her presumed return. So the lines are both tragically prophetic and dramatically momentary. And the hesitation, as to whether 'deceav'd' and 'failing' are absolute or particular, is resolved here by our realizing that there are not in fact two paths at all, but only one. For Eve to be wrong about anything (even that she would soon be back) is for her to be wrong about everything. Before the Fall, the distinction of absolute or particular failing does not exist. Once deception and failure have arrived, then they have arrived absolutely. It is the hesitating syntax which makes the point, and resolves itself.

Mr. Stein has drawn attention to the delicate balance of present innocence with potential danger when Eve leaves Raphael and Adam:

> With Goddess-like demeanour forth she went;
> Not unattended, for on her as Queen

> A pomp of winning Graces waited still,
> And from about her shot Darts of desire
> Into all Eyes to wish her still in sight. (VIII. 59–63)

'She leaves', says Mr. Stein, 'under circumstances that emphasize (and create the opportunity for emphasizing) at once her genuine charms, her potentially dangerous charms (the "darts of desire"), and her relations (according to the scale of creation) with Adam.'[1]

It is true that the 'Darts of desire' are potentially dangerous.[2] But the point about the delicate balance of danger and innocence could best be made by reference, first, to the rhythm (which emphatically juxtaposes 'shot Darts'), and, second, to the syntax:

> And from about her shot Darts of desire
> Into all Eyes to wish her still in sight.

The balance is in the hesitation. At first, *desire* seems absolute, and as such potentially dangerous and prophetic of the Fall:

> Carnal desire enflaming, hee on Eve
> Began to cast lascivious Eyes, she him
> As wantonly repaid. (IX. 1013–15)

And the hesitation is maintained by the delaying phrase 'into all Eyes'—after which, and only after which, is the *desire* defined as still innocent: 'to wish her still in sight'. Richardson noticed the ambivalence of the syntax, and hurried to protect Eve's honour: 'This passage must be pointed Thus, as in *Milton*'s Editions; as Some have done it, it makes Wild work. Darts of desire but Only to Wish her Stay.'[3]

The potential danger, then, is expressed in the potential syntax. We are shown a path which Adam and Eve might take (and which tragically we know they will take), but they have not yet taken it. Potential danger, but still actual innocence. So the syntax is resolved into innocence, with

[1] *Answerable Style*, p. 91.

[2] Adam was 'here onely weake / Against the charm of Beauties powerful glance' (VIII. 532–3).

[3] p. 356.

justice to Eve. But the hesitation about 'desire' is essential to the effect—if it is equivocal, that is because it thereby provides a perfect mirror for the equivocal position of Adam and Eve before the Fall (if they could fall, were they not already in some sense fallen?). The lines admirably fulfil Dr. Davie's wishes for poetic syntax: 'a movement of syntax can render, immediately present, the curve of destiny through a life or the path of an energy through the mind.'[1]

How, and how admirably, the lines do so, is clear if we substitute a more usual word-order, one that does not deliberately delay:

> And from about her shot into all Eyes
> Darts of desire to wish her still in sight.

The innocence of 'desire' is there established too quickly. The subtle effect depended on subtle syntax, and also on the opportunity for legitimate surprise that is offered by the line-endings. Dr. Davie finds that the line-endings are poorly used. Just how effective they really are is shown by William Forde's *The True Spirit of Milton's Versification* (1831), which quaintly rearranges the verse into sense-units: 'The *Lines* will now represent the natural division of every sentence into its component Members', so that 'the reader may attend solely to the sense and the harmonious order of the words, without feeling any embarrassment from the contrariety between the linear division, and the meaning of the language'.[2] But it is exactly this 'contrariety' which Milton uses to enforce his meaning, and when this 'embarrassment' disappears, so does the precision and the emphasis. A neat modern example is Mr. Whaler's observation that at one point Milton's lines may be slid along into a different iambic pattern, and with very different effect. Thus Milton wrote:

> But wherefore thou alone? wherefore with thee
> Came not all Hell broke loose? is pain to them
> Less pain, less to be fled, or thou then they
> Less hardie to endure? courageous Chief,

[1] *Articulate Energy*, p. 157.

[2] pp. xxix, xxxiii.

The first in flight from pain, had'st thou alleg'd
To thy deserted host this cause of flight,
Thou surely hadst not come sole fugitive. (IV. 917–23)

Mr. Whaler[1] slides the pattern along, and the result is fascinating, not so much numerologically (Mr. Whaler's concern) as critically:

But wherefore thou alone?
Wherefore with thee came not all Hell broke loose?
Is pain to them less pain, less to be fled,
Or thou then they less hardie to endure?
Courageous Chief, the first in flight from pain,
Had'st thou alleg'd to thy deserted host
This cause of flight, thou surely hadst not come
Sole fugitive.

Milton's lines have become eighteenth-century Miltonics. The surge of the verse has gone, and been replaced by the dullness of three questions that fall neatly at the ends of the lines. The playing of the syntax against the metre has disappeared, and with it has gone the emphatic placing of 'Less pain' and 'Less hardie' at the opening of the lines, and above all the great weight which the last line of the speech received by being the only one where the sense-unit met and clinched the metre.

Let me return from the 'hesitations', and their dependence on the skilful use of line-endings, to the point at which it was necessary to explain them: the suggestive mingling of the senses in the harmony of Paradise. An eighteenth-century editor might well have objected to Eve's lines:

Not distant far from thence a murmuring sound
Of waters issu'd from a Cave and spread
Into a liquid Plain, then stood unmov'd
Pure as th' expanse of Heav'n . . . (IV. 453–6)

We all know what this means, but it does say that the *sound* 'spread into a liquid Plain . . .'. Is this just carelessness? Or is there a reason why Milton treats the water as sound?

[1] *Counterpoint and Symbol*, pp. 20–21.

First, we must remember Milton's recurring insistence that sound is a movement of the air, that an air is the air. We sense how all the different movements of the air, including sounds, blend together in Paradise:

for his sleep
Was Aerie light, from pure digestion bred,
And temperat vapors bland, which th'only sound
Of leaves and fuming rills, Aurora's fan,
Lightly dispers'd, and the shrill Matin Song
Of Birds on every bough. (V. 3–8)

'Sound' as 'air', then, in the lines of Eve under discussion. But what is there in the context that explains the further mingling of the air with water?

Eve awakes, and gazes like Narcissus into the lake, which is 'pure as th' expanse of Heav'n',

the cleer
Smooth Lake, that to me seemd another Skie. (IV. 458–9)

Upon this mirroring of the airy sky in the lake depends the whole important episode. But perhaps 'mirroring' judges the situation more knowledgeably than Eve could—say rather, indistinguishability: 'Uncertain which, in Ocean or in Air' (III. 76). Milton insists on the indistinguishable commingling not only by the explicit comparisons, but also by the syntactical mingling in a 'sound . . . spread into a liquid Plain'. It is not entirely accidental that we might talk of the *fluidity* of such syntax.

That this is Milton's creation rather than mine is made clear if we notice how he does not rely upon the syntax and the explicit comparisons alone, but uses for the water the diction with which he elsewhere presents the creation of the airy sky—*liquid*, *pure*, and *expanse*:

and God made
The Firmament, expanse of liquid, pure,
Transparent, Elemental Air. (VII. 263–5)[1]

[1] Cp. 'Nor in thir liquid texture mortal wound
Receive, no more then can the fluid Aire.' (VI. 348–9)

Of course 'the liquid air' is a commonplace,[1] but it is one of great use and importance when Eve as it were regards herself as Narcissus—one of the most poignantly significant of her appearances before the Fall. Milton brings this commonplace to life by blurring the distinction between air and water in his syntax.

Bentley was shocked by the lines which I have just quoted from the opening of Book v, describing Adam waking to the vapours and sounds of Paradise. He took exception to the phrase 'th'only sound of leaves and fuming rills': 'What's that which follows, *The sound of fuming Rills*?'[2] Newton followed Pearce and said sensibly: 'They do not make a noise as *fuming*, but only as *rills*.'[3] True enough. But it is not necessary to believe that Milton was unaware of the strangely lovely suggestion which Bentley noticed.

To handle syntax with such various control is not what one would expect from a poet who was callous to the intrinsic nature of English. The syntax moves between the quiet poles of the power that can launch an 'adventrous Song', and the delicacy that augments the song by tincture and reflection. 'Milton', said Hopkins, 'is the great master of sequence of phrase'; and R. W. Dixon, agreeing, offered an apt image in describing the Miltonic style as 'a deliberate unrolling as if of some vast material'.[4] The more one looks closely at Milton's word-order, the less truth there seems to be in Mr. Eliot's remark[5] that 'the syntax is determined by the musical significance, by the auditory imagination, rather than by the attempt to follow actual speech or thought'.

III. SILENT YET SPAKE

It is not only Milton's word-order that invites Richardson's comment: 'Though the Text does not Say it, the Reader will from the Words naturally be led to imagine . . .'.[6] Milton

[1] John Arthos quotes thirty-eight examples from Empedocles to Genest (*The Language of Natural Description in 18th Century Poetry*, 1949, pp. 237–40).

[2] p. 146. [3] i. 311. [4] Letters of 13 June and 25 Sept. 1878.

[5] *On Poetry and Poets*, p. 142. [6] p. 63.

is adept at releasing the subtle energies not only of word against word, but also within the word. Mr. Prince states the fact from which discussion must begin: 'In Milton's epic poetry there is an incessant, sometimes obtrusive, activity of mind at the level of verbal wit: there is play upon words, sometimes in puns, sometimes in emphasizing the jingling qualities of words of different or kindred meaning.'[1]

Yet *jingling* is liable to suggest too trivial a tone. When Adam cries out after the Fall, 'O Eve, in evil hour thou didst give eare / To that false Worm' (IX. 1067–8), his cry proclaims that the word evil is derived from Eve, and that evil derives from her. That is more of a knell than a jingle. We can see the difference if we think of the line from Sylvester's Du Bartas which Milton may have had in mind: 'O Lot! alas! what lot hast thou elect!'[2] Milton's line has an altogether different resonance and depth, mainly because it *is* a 'jingle' and not a pun: the distance from *Lot* to *lot* would be too great for the epic, and in any case leaves us feeling 'how clever', rather than—as with *Eve* . . . *evil*—'how wounding'.

It is a knell, too, that sounds in the relentless insistence that the *Fall* was the source of the *false*. Adam saw how the 'false Worm' had lied in prophecy:

> true in our Fall,
> False in our promis'd Rising. (IX. 1069–70)

And the Fall is the source of all fault:

> So will fall
> Hee and his faithless Progenie: whose fault? (III. 95–96)

And it is the source of all failing—God makes this explicit:

> And Spirits, both them who stood & them who faild;
> Freely they stood who stood, and fell who fell. (III. 101–2)

This was more than Bentley could take, and he emended 'faild' to 'fell'. But the rhyme may well be meant to be gratingly unnerving, as it is when Adam speaks:

[1] *The Italian Element*, p. 123.

[2] Suggested by Charles Dunster in 1800 (*Considerations on Milton's Early Reading*, p. 14).

Set over all his Works, which in our Fall,
For us created, needs with us must faile. (IX. 941–2)

Such tolling of a word is powerful in its simplicity; its frequency in *Paradise Lost* is reason enough for supposing that Milton was a witty as well as a profound poet, and for looking at some of the more unobtrusive forms which his wit takes.[1] Mr. Prince adeptly reminds us that ingenuity is everywhere in Milton: 'The play upon words and the metaphysical or logical conceits are not indeed alien to this epic style, for ingenuity is here omnipresent in one form or another: it is present in the artificial word-order and in the music of the verse no less than in the assiduous search for what is astounding in thought and image and emotion.'[2]

At its best, such ingenuity can act as a silent pun, where the vitality of the epic is maintained through the pun, and the dignity of the epic through the silence. Mr. Empson declared that 'the most obvious case where neither Bentley nor Pearce can approve Milton's method is where he uses a serious secret pun':

The Birds thir quire apply; aires, vernal aires,
Breathing the smell of field and grove, attune
The trembling leaves. (IV. 264–6)

Bentley insisted that '*Air*, when taken for the *Element*, has no Plural Number, in *Greek*, *Latin*, or *English*; where *Airs* signify *Tunes*. Therefore he must give it here, . . . AIR ATTUNES'.[3] Mr. Empson's comment is beautiful and precise:

It is strange that Bentley should actually use the word *tunes*, and then quote the word *attunes*, and still not see there is a pun. The airs attune the leaves because the air itself is as enlivening as an air; the trees and wild flowers that are smelt on the air match, as if they caused,

[1] Aubrey: Milton was 'Extreme pleasant in his conversation . . . but Satyricall. (He pronounced the letter R (*littera canina*) very hard—a certaine signe of a Satyricall Witt—*from John Dreyden*.)'

[2] *The Italian Element*, pp. 123–4. In *The French Biblical Epic in the 17th Century* (pp. 210, 214, 217), Dr. R. A. Sayce mentions the word-play of Gamon, of Pierre de Saint-Louis, and of Saint-Amant.

[3] p. 115 (misnumbered 215).

as if they were caused by, the birds and leaves that are heard on the air; nature, because of a pun, becomes a single organism. A critical theory is powerful indeed when it can blind its holders to so much beauty.[1]

Yet Mr. John Crowe Ransom doubted if there was a pun, and moreover thought it would be bad if there were:

> This one would be a very disagreeable pun. The birds make tunes but do not need an external apparatus, they furnish their own choir; then the breezes follow suit, but they have to do it by attuning the leaves, just as it might be said that Pan makes music by attuning the reed; the airs do this, but they are airs in the sense of breezes; and there are no airs in the sense of tunes until they do. To discover presently that the airs were already tunes, and did not need the assistance of the leaves, is to feel that the poet has been teasing us, and really the poet, even if he is Milton, cannot afford to give us that impression.[2]

Of course *breezes* is the main sense. And perhaps, in order to meet Mr. Ransom, it would be best to abandon the word 'pun'. *Airs* does not present us with two meanings both of which make literal sense, and so it is not perhaps a pun. But it offers a main meaning—breezes—while at the same time anticipating the music, lending to the breezes an enhancing suggestion. The effect is one of tincture or reflection, not of fusion. A prose paraphrase would have to offer *breezes* as the sense; but such a paraphrase would lose the beautiful suggestion that in Paradise the airs were magically musical. In essence, the beauty is one of anticipation—*prolepsis* is surely the key-figure throughout *Paradise Lost*, in the fable itself, in allusion, in simile, and even in syntax and word-play. If this Paradisal moment—as Mr. Ransom says—teases us, it teases us out of thought:

> Heard melodies are sweet, but those unheard
> Are sweeeter.

In any case, if Mr. Ransom finds the suggestion of music here disagreeable, he ought to blame Milton rather than Empson. It was not the critic of 1935, but (as it happens)

[1] *Some Versions*, p. 157.
[2] *The Southern Review* (1938), iv. 326.

Patrick Hume in 1695, who first pointed out the music here: 'Soft Breaths and gentle Gales . . . move the Trees trembling Leaves into a Tune, consorting with the Feather'd Quire. *Aires* seem here to be meant of Musical Airs, sweet and yet brisk, which have their Derivation of the Greek, the Air; for all Musick, either Vocal or Instrumental, is but the beating and breaking of the Air.'[1]

Hume's note is perfectly poised, in that it gives the proper primacy to the literal meaning 'gentle Gales' before it offers the enhancing suggestion that *aires* is 'meant of Musical Airs'.

That Milton's first editor should so anticipate Mr. Empson is striking evidence of how there is more than one 'traditional' way of reading Milton. In many ways, the man who is thought of as a super-subtle modernist is closer in spirit to Milton's audience than is the nineteenth-century scholar.

Added to which, we do not need Hume's note, welcome though it is, to support the conjecture. There is support elsewhere in the poem. The enhancing association of airs (breezes) with music comes again, and once more with the *Quire* and the *scents*:

> forth came the human pair
> And joynd thir vocal Worship to the Quire
> Of Creatures wanting voice, that done, partake
> The season, prime for sweetest Sents and Aires. (IX. 197–200)

In a sense, that means only breezes, but the parallel—which would otherwise be a very odd coincidence—suggests that once again the airs are tinged with unheard melody. And the scents and bird-songs of Paradise, all carried by the air, blend again at Eve's nuptials:

> Joyous the Birds; fresh Gales and gentle Aires
> Whisper'd it to the Woods, and from thir Wings
> Flung Rose, flung Odours from the spicie Shrub,
> Disporting, till the amorous Bird of Night
> Sung Spousal. (VIII. 515–19)

[1] p. 140. James Paterson in 1744 followed Hume: 'Gentle Gales . . . Here, Musical Tunes' (*A Commentary on P.L.*, p. 304). The play on *airs* would hardly have escaped a seventeenth-century reader—see, for example, Crashaw's 'Musicks Duell'.

If, like Mr. Ransom, one finds this disagreeable, it will seem a pity that Milton used it so often. But it is possible to feel that, once Milton had described their choir, 'Never again would birds' song be the same.' It is possible to find such a serious secret pun a triumph—and a characteristic triumph.

The only other time that Milton uses *airs* in the poem, he associates it with music by the reflection from *cadence*. It might have been pedantic to use *cadence* for what Browning's Duke curtly called 'the dropping of the daylight in the West', but with the help of *airs* Milton momentarily lends the musical beauty of a dying fall to evening in Eden:

> Now was the Sun in Western cadence low
> From Noon, and gentle Aires due at thir hour
> To fan the Earth now wak'd . . . (x. 92–94)

And it is clear that the effect of *cadence* is intended, from the precision with which Milton presented a lullaby of rising and falling:

> The sound of blustring winds, which all night long
> Had rous'd the Sea, now with hoarse cadence lull
> Sea-faring men orewatcht. (II. 286–8)[1]

The lyrical beauty of 'Western cadence low' is comparable to the more famous 'charm of earliest Birds', where the beauty of *charm* is not all subsumed into the dialect-word for 'the noise of birds'.[2]

Similarly, it would be mistaken to suppose that Milton is merely substituting a remoter word for the usual one when

[1] *O.E.D.*: *Cadence*: 'The literal sense is "action or mode of falling, fall", and in this sense it was used by 17th century writers [the only examples cited are 1613, 1660, and Milton]; but at an early period the word was in Italian appropriated to the musical or rhythmical fall of the voice, and in this sense occurs as early as Chaucer.' In her valuable article 'Some Notes on Milton's Use of Words' (*E. & S.*, 1924, p. 102), Elizabeth Holmes brings out the double meaning in the lines from Book II above, but is less explicit about the 'Western cadence' ('the sense is the primary Latin one, and I know of no contemporary use of "cadence" which has such full concrete beauty').

[2] On this, and related points, see Professor C. L. Wrenn, 'The Language of Milton', *Studies Presented to Karl Brunner* (1957), *Wiener Beiträge zur Englischen Philologie*, lxv, pp. 256–7.

the serpent is described as he approaches Eve: 'Then *voluble* and bold, now hid, now seen' (IX. 436). Of course the sense is Latinate, and it insists on the coiled movement of the snake. But we are to sense a reminder or a hint in the word too. The snake is to be all too voluble in the commoner sense ('So gloz'd the Tempter, and his Proem tun'd').[1] It is common enough for Milton to find moral likenesses in the corporeal, and particularly when he describes the snake:

> In Labyrinth of many a round self-rowld,
> His head the midst, well stor'd with suttle wiles. (IX. 183–4)[2]

And that we are ominously to sense what is to come (the English sense of *voluble*) as well as watch the snake at this moment (the Latin sense) is suggested by the spelling and stress—vóluble—which are those which Milton gives to the English rather than the Latin.[3]

Nor are such effects rare. The snake has been described as 'insinuating' (IV. 348), where once again the physical meaning vibrates with the moral one, which is well established in Milton's day. As Macaulay finely said in praise of Milton, 'New forms of beauty start at once into existence, and all the burial-places of the memory give up their dead.'[4]

[1] The main meaning by the seventeenth century is clearly 'glib, fluent' (*O.E.D.* II). *O.E.D.* 3 is 'moving rapidly and easily, esp. with a gliding or undulating movement'; the quoted examples before Milton are 1589 and 1608. It is interesting that the 1608 quotation should be from Topsell's *Serpents*, and that by applying it to the *tongue*, his usage should bridge the two applications, to Satan's movement and to his speech: '. . . voluble; neither is there any beast that moveth the tongue so speedily.' Elizabeth Holmes does not mention this instance, and simply contrasts *P.L.*, IV. 594 (rolling), with *S.A.*, 1307 (fluent).

[2] The emblem is traditional, as Arnold Williams shows from the commentators on Genesis (*The Common Expositor*, p. 115).

[3] (*a*) 'His message will be short and *voluble*' (*S.A.*, 1307).

(*b*) 'whither the prime Orb,
Incredible how swift, had thither rowl'd
Diurnal, or this less *volubil* Earth
By shorter flight to th' East . . . (IV. 592–5)

The stress of (*b*) cannot be proved; but I follow Elizabeth Holmes in thinking that here 'the spelling and accenting appear indicative of a conscious return to Latin' (p. 121). The Latin pronunciation (volūbilis) seems more likely—the other rhythm would be very jagged.

[4] *Literary and Historical Essays* (1934), p. 10.

I take from the eighteenth century my final example of how Milton releases enhancing suggestions from the burial-places of memory. In the closing lines of the poem, the cherubim are described as

> Gliding meteorous, as Ev'ning Mist
> Ris'n from a River o're the marish glides. (XII. 629–30)[1]

Richardson drew attention to the derivation of *meteorous* (raised on high): ' as a Meteor, Aloft . . . So the Word Signifies, Gliding above the Surface . . .'.[2] But with his frequent acumen, he did not leave the matter there, but brought out just why we must be aware of precisely what the word means: 'So the Word Signifies, Gliding above the Surface, in Opposition to the Black, Low-Creeping Mist in which *Satan* Wrapt himself' when he invaded the garden:

> In with the River sunk, and with it rose
> Satan involv'd in rising Mist . . .
>
> thus wrapt in mist
> Of midnight vapor glide obscure . . .
>
> Like a black mist low creeping, he held on
> His midnight search . . . (IX. 74–75, 158–9, 180–1)

In the difference between 'evening' and 'midnight', in the difference between a mist that is meteorous and one that is low-creeping, is all the difference between the angels who stood and those who fell, those who drive out and those who are driven. And the pointer to such a superb use of cross-reference is precision of language.

IV. WORDS, ACTIONS ALL INFECT

With the Fall of Man, language falls too. The prophecy which Sin makes include words, as was inevitable:

> Till I in Man residing through the Race,
> His thoughts, his looks, words, actions all infect.[3] (X. 607–8)

[1] K. Svendsen has an informative but knotty discussion of the lore in these lines (*Milton and Science*, 1956, pp. 105–12).

[2] p. 533.

[3] Arnold Williams summarizes the commentators on Genesis: 'In the beginning man was given a perfect language to go with the perfect nature in which he was

So one of the reasons why Milton often uses 'words in their proper and primary signification' (Newton) is because he can thereby re-create something of the pre-lapsarian state of language. Mr. Stein has brilliantly drawn attention to the play with the word 'error' in the account of the river in Paradise, 'With mazie error under pendant shades' (IV. 239):

> Here, before the Fall, the word *error* argues, from its original meaning, for the order in irregularity, for the rightness in wandering—before the concept of error is introduced into man's world and comes to signify wrong wandering. Back of the phrase are the echoes from hell, Belial's precious thoughts that wander, and the debates of the philosophical angels 'in wandring mazes lost'.[1]

Error here is not exactly a pun, since it means only 'wandering'—but the 'only' is a different thing from an absolutely simple use of the word, since the evil meaning is consciously and ominously excluded. Rather than the meaning being simply 'wandering', it is 'wandering (not error)'. Certainly the word is a reminder of the Fall, in that it takes us back to a time when there were no infected words because there were no infected actions.

Not that one can *prove* that the word is not simple Latinism. But 'error' is frequent enough in its fallen meaning in the poem for such Latinism to be of a powerfully and unusually obtuse kind: 'I also err'd in overmuch admiring'; 'I rue that errour now'; 'inmost powers made erre'.[2] And the same prelapsarian play occurs during the Creation, when it is fortified with *serpent*: the waters are 'with Serpent errour wandring' (VII. 302). It is surely easier to believe in a slightly ingenious Milton than in one who could be so strangely absent-minded as to use both 'serpent' and 'error' without in some way invoking the Fall.[3] And when Milton uses 'error' elsewhere than in *Paradise Lost*, it always has the fallen meaning.

created. Then, as a result of sin, this perfect language was, like human nature, corrupted' (*The Common Expositor*, p. 228).

[1] *Answerable Style*, pp. 66–67.

[2] IX. 1178, 1180–1, 1048–9.

[3] Elizabeth Holmes: 'Milton marks and beautifies his usage by linking the Latin-derived word with the native in a way that is frequent with him . . . "serpent" . . . is really a present participle, meaning "crawling".' (*E. & S.*, 1924, p. 105.)

Many of the Latinisms involve just this choice: is Milton reaching back to an earlier purity—which we are to contrast with what has happened to the word, and the world, since? Or is he simply being forgetful? The answer is likely to depend on one's general estimate of Milton. When in Paradise we hear the 'liquid Lapse of murmuring Streams' (VIII. 263), the meaning may be 'falling (not the Fall)'. Certainly many of Milton's finest effects come from just this invoking of what is then deliberately excluded: 'Not that faire field of Enna . . .', or the story of the fall of Mulciber, or the beauty of the bower:

> In shadier Bower
> More sacred and sequesterd, though but feignd,
> Pan or Silvanus never slept, nor Nymph,
> Nor Faunus haunted. (IV. 705–8)

The Miltonic style is very much of a piece, and the habits so fruitfully at work in the allusions may well be the same as those that inspire the words themselves. To invoke, and then to exclude; so that a 'Lapse' becomes 'falling, not the Fall'.[1] Milton uses 'lapse' enough times for the Fall for it to be improbable that such a meaning is merely forgotten: 'I will renew his lapsed powers'; 'Man whom they triumph'd once lapst'; 'thy original lapse'; 'Which would but lead me to a worse relapse, And heavier fall'.[2] How tragically far we are from the 'liquid Lapse of murmuring Streams'. The irrevocable Fall has degraded language too, and turned those innocent notes to tragic.

The Paradisal state of language is naturally most clear in descriptions of Paradise, where there is not yet any grave distinction between 'luxuriant' and 'luxurious':

[1] Arnold Stein mentions a pun, but without comment (*Answerable Style*, p. 145). Book I, chapter xi of *De Doctrina Christiana* is 'De lapsu primorum parentum'. *Lapse* was specifically, though rarely, used in English for the Fall (*O.E.D.* 2b, from 1659). *O.E.D.* 6, 'a gliding, flow (of water)', begins with Milton's line. My emphasis is different from that of Elizabeth Holmes: 'Milton's sense in the text is the simple concrete one of "a falling or gliding" ' (*E. & S.*, 1924, p. 108).

[2] III. 175–6; X. 571–2; XII. 83; IV. 100–1.

the mantling Vine
Layes forth her purple Grape, and gently creeps
Luxuriant . . . (IV. 258–60)

The work under our labour grows,
Luxurious by restraint . . . (IX. 208–9)

Both words are innocent; but both remind us ominously that innocence will soon be gone, and that instead of luxurious plants we shall know of 'luxurious Cities', 'wealth and luxurie', 'luxurious wealth', 'luxurie and riot'.[1]

Once again, outside *Paradise Lost* Milton does not use the word in its 'unfallen' sense. (And the *O.E.D.* shows how old and powerful is the meaning 'unchaste, excessive, voluptuous'). In the same way the 'wantonness' of Eden, or of its inhabitants, is neither mere description nor moral condemnation: it is 'mere description (not moral condemnation)'.

For Nature here
Wantond as in her prime, and plaid at will
Her Virgin Fancies. (V. 294–6)

Such wantonness is still virginal (Herrick's 'cleanly-wantonness'), as it is in the 'wanton growth' of the branches, or —poignantly—in the 'wanton ringlets' of Eve.[2] But in Hell we have already heard the fallen word, have heard of 'wanton rites' and 'wanton passions';[3] and Satan brings fallen wantonness to the seduction of Eve, so that the word is infected before our eyes:

and of his tortuous Traine
Curld many a wanton wreath in sight of Eve,
To lure her Eye. (IX. 516–18)

So it is not long after the Fall that Adam and Eve become liable to the grimmer meaning:

hee on Eve
Began to cast lascivious Eyes, she him
As wantonly repaid. (IX. 1013–15)

[1] I. 498, 722; XI. 784, 711.
[2] IV. 629, 306.
[3] I. 414, 454.

But though clearest in descriptions of Paradise, such play is also found elsewhere. It is easy to point to, though admittedly hard to substantiate. Take *grateful*, for instance.[1] Sometimes it has the sense of 'thankful', sometimes of 'pleasing' (both are common seventeenth-century meanings). Perhaps Milton's fondness for the word is a reflection of the fact that in a pre-lapsarian state there would be no distinction of this kind. Adam and Eve were thankful for what pleased them, and being thankful is itself a pleasure. So Milton clings to the ancient meaning not out of pedantry, but because its original unity represents the innocent integrity of Paradise.

Certainly ingratitude is the great theme of the poem. Adam, Eve, and Satan are all guilty of it, and it occasions some of the most moving passages in the poem. And Milton brings out the essential connexion between ancient and modern meanings by sometimes leaving it uncertain which he has chosen, or at any rate tingeing the one with the other:

> So many grateful Altars I would reare
> Of grassie Terfe, and pile up every Stone
> Of lustre from the brook, in memorie,
> Or monument to Ages, and thereon
> Offer sweet smelling Gumms & Fruits and Flours. (XI. 323–7)

'Grateful' there is primarily gratitude; but it is clear from 'lustre' and 'sweet smelling' that the altars will also be pleasing. To make any such distinction is to show the infection of the Fall.

Is the steam of Abel's sacrifice pleasant as well as thankfully received?

> His Offring soon propitious Fire from Heav'n
> Consum'd with nimble glance, and grateful steame. (XI. 441–2)

This pristine interchangeability is clearer in the earlier Paradisal scene of offering,

> when all things that breath,
> From th' Earths great Altar send up silent praise

[1] Arnold Stein draws attention to the word; his comment is deft but rather overcomplicated (*Answerable Style*, p. 60).

To the Creator, and his Nostrils fill
With gratefull Smell. (IX. 194–7)

Perhaps the most beautiful of such moments is when Noah leaves the ark, and through the equivocal fluidity of the syntax, his gratitude to Heaven is itself pleasing to Heaven:

Then with uplifted hands, and eyes devout,
Grateful to Heav'n, over his head beholds
A dewie Cloud, and in the Cloud a Bow . . . (XI. 859–61)

It is this recovery of innocence which makes Milton choose a pristine meaning even when elsewhere his poem shows him fully aware of the later degrading development. It is not pedantry, but the beauty and aptness of Prometheus, which makes him imitate Latin in his description of Eve

with such Gardning Tools as Art yet rude,
Guiltless of fire had formd, or Angels brought. (IX. 391–2)

Guiltless because of the story of Prometheus, as Richardson insisted.[1] Eve still has a few moments before she is too like Pandora,

O too like
In sad event, when to the unwiser Son
Of Japhet brought by Hermes, she ensnar'd
Mankind with her faire looks, to be aveng'd
On him who had stole Joves authentic fire. (IV. 715–19)

Fire comes with the Fall:

ere this diurnal Starr
Leave cold the Night, how we his gather'd beams
Reflected, may with matter sere foment,
Or by collision of two bodies grinde
The Air attrite to Fire. (X. 1069–73)

All of which means that 'guiltless' is very much more than a schoolmasterly way of saying 'with no experience of'.[2]

[1] p. 410.

[2] *O.E.D.* 3 = 'Having no acquaintance, dealings, or familiarity with, no experience or use of (something)'. It quotes Milton first, and adds Dryden and Shenstone (both in imitation). 'Guilt' and 'guilty' come eleven times in *P.L.*; and Milton's four other uses of 'guiltless' all mean 'innocent'.

What happens in the narrative is reflected in what happens to the words. Contrast Adam's two trances, the first given by God during the creation of Eve, the second the satiety after the Fall:

> there gentle sleep
> First found me, and with soft oppression seis'd
> My drousèd sense . . . (VIII. 287–9)

and

> The solace of thir sin, till dewie sleep
> Oppress'd them, wearied with thir amorous play. (IX. 1044–5)

The innocence of the first moment makes 'oppression' neutral, a soft and gentle pressure.[1] With the second moment, Adam and Eve are 'oppress'd' as we would understand the word—and the state. And what is in store for the world is foretold by Michael: 'So violence proceeded, and Oppression' (XI. 667–8).

Before sin was, *absolution* was no more than completion:

> what cause
> Mov'd the Creator in his holy Rest
> Through all Eternitie so late to build
> In Chaos, and the work begun, how soon
> Absolv'd. (VII. 90–94)

Akenside imitated this usage, and rightly incurred Johnson's blame: 'And the pedant surely intrudes—but when was blank verse without pedantry?—when he tells how "Planets absolve the stated round of Time".'[2] Certainly Akenside's disregard for what 'absolve' usually means is no more than pedantic; but is Milton deliberately setting aside, and asking us to see that he has set aside, the application to sin because he is describing a sinless world? At any rate, it seems relevant

[1] Such a usage is apparently unique in *O.E.D.* Although *oppression* 1. seems to be neutral ('the action of pressing or weighing down'), its instances are affected by their contexts: a. 1490, Caxton 'righte grete violence, by the opressions of the shippes'; b. *Richard II*, 'make their Syre Stoupe with oppression of their prodigall weight'; c. Milton's line; and d. an imitation of it by Thomson.

[2] *Lives of the Poets*, ed. Hill, iii. 418.

that with all these words Milton makes full use of the fallen meanings:

> His crime makes guiltie all his Sons, thy merit
> Imputed shall absolve them who renounce
> Thir own both righteous and unrighteous deeds. (III. 290–2)

At its simplest, such a device need involve no more than the contrast between two current meanings. What is 're-morse'? The remorse of God and his good angels is pity, a different thing from the remorse of the ill-doers. Satan, Adam, and Eve all feel remorse; but Raphael's emotion deserves the pure meaning: how may he relate

> without remorse
> The ruin of so many glorious once
> And perfet while they stood. (V. 566–8)

Neither Raphael nor Michael *could* feel remorse in its fallen sense, and the very inapplicability of that sense is a measure of their goodness, contrasted with the 'sinful Pair':

> Hast thee, and from the Paradise of God
> Without remorse drive out the sinful Pair,
> From hallowd ground th' unholie . . . (XI. 104–6)

And is 'liberality' a good or a bad thing? The liberality of God is different from that of Eve, because it is directed by a sense of man's 'well being':

> how may I
> Adore thee, Author of this Universe,
> And all this good to man, for whose well being
> So amply, and with hands so liberal
> Thou hast provided all things. (VIII. 359–63)

But Eve's liberality is darkened and infected, as is her recompense:

> In recompence (for such compliance bad
> Such recompence best merits) from the bough
> She gave him of that fair enticing Fruit
> With liberal hand. (IX. 994–7)

Through such delicate anticipations and echoes, Milton creates a style which is not only grand but also suggestive, as the eighteenth-century commentators saw. It does not seem true that 'the mind that invented Milton's Grand Style had renounced the English language'.[1] On the contrary, he triumphantly combined what might well seem to be incompatible greatnesses. His style is not only grand in its explicitness, but also—as Arnold insisted—pregnant and allusive: 'Milton charges himself so full with thought, imagination, knowledge, that his style will hardly contain them. He is too full-stored to show us in much detail one conception, one piece of knowledge; he just shows it to us in a pregnant allusive way, and then he presses on to another'.[2]

[1] F. R. Leavis, *Revaluation*, p. 52.

[2] *On Translating Homer*, III.

4. Simile and Cross-reference

THE twentieth-century criticism of Milton's similes is one of the most useful recent discussions of Milton's style. So much so, that one is doubtful about the need to enter again into the question. Yet no account of Milton's style may omit some mention of the similes, which are characteristic in their power and beauty. And the best of the recent criticism is in articles which have not been reprinted, and which may therefore not be as well known as they ought to be. Moreover, the eighteenth-century comments on the similes are often of interest and value.

But first my debt to recent critics. The argument about the similes is in essence a simple one, and analogous to the argument about Milton's use of words: are they epic similes which fasten on a broad point of resemblance and then drift beautifully away? Or are they more closely related to the poem? It was Mr. James Whaler who provided the earliest and fullest discussion of this important question.

Of his four articles, the most useful is 'The Miltonic Simile'.[1] It is long, detailed, and in some ways brilliant—though the brilliance is likely to be obscured by its unnecessary mathematical symbols. Mr. Whaler's knowledge of classical epic simile gives authority to his main point about Milton, which is to insist on how often his similes are pro-

[1] *P.M.L.A.*, 1931. The others are: *Modern Philology*, 1931, studying the compounding and distribution of the similes; *Journal of English and Germanic Philology*, 1931, on their grammatical nexus; and *P.M.L.A.*, 1932, which discusses the scarcity of animal similes in *P.L.*

leptic. It may at first seem that a particular simile has no special point to make—but again and again we find that it anticipates a later devĕlopment of the fable. Of course this was made possible by the nature of his story, which is one of the most famous in the world. But it is certain that to appreciate many of his similes, it is necessary to bring the whole of the story, not just the immediate moment, to bear on it. Mr. Whaler's position is a simple one, though the working out of it is subtle: 'A typically complex Miltonic simile directs each detail to some application in the fable. . . . Milton's similes are organically related to a degree beyond those of his epic predecessors.'[1] He tackles almost all the similes, and for the most part his commentary is not only exciting but trustworthy—though like everybody he sometimes indulges in unsubstantiated guesses.

Mr. Whaler's argument was developed and modified in a clear and modest article by Mr. L. D. Lerner in *Essays in Criticism* (1954). Mr. Lerner is lucidly sceptical about the ingenious excesses to which a modern critic is liable,[2] and his exposition is valuable for its moderation. Subsequent critics have contributed to the debate, and it seems now to be generally accepted that most, or at any rate many, of Milton's similes are 'organically related'.[3] Though Waldock gave a snort: 'The effort to find a continuous relevance in Milton's similes may succeed on occasion, but it is an effort, it seems to me, that can easily overreach itself.'[4] Certainly—all critical efforts can easily overreach themselves. The crux is the phrase 'may succeed on occasion'. On how many occasions? To answer that would require a very much more detailed discussion than Waldock provides. He was really

[1] *P.M.L.A.* (1931), xlvi. 1034, 1037.

[2] Mr. Empson's remarks on the similes (in *Some Versions*) are among the least convincing parts of his essay.

[3] Dr. Broadbent has many shrewd and subtle things to say in *Some Graver Subject*, and in 'Milton and Arnold' (*E. in C.*, 1956). Mrs. MacCaffrey has some interesting comments in chapter v of *P.L. as 'Myth'*. Mr. Peter studies the decline in the quality of the similes as the poem progresses (*A Critique of P.L.*, pp. 55–58).

[4] *P.L. and Its Critics* (1947), p. 143.

grumbling about Mr. Empson, and seems not to have been aware of Mr. Whaler's articles.

But what if we move back from the twentieth century to Milton's earliest commentators? Would they have read Mr. Whaler with smiling astonishment? Or do we find once again that in some ways they are strangely modernist?

Mr. Whaler himself referred to what is the best of the eighteenth-century discussions of the similes, *An Essay upon Milton's Imitations of the Ancients* (1741)—though he mistakenly attributed it to Newton, who quoted it in his edition. The *Essay* is apparently by C. Falconer, according to a contemporary attribution in one of the Bodleian Library copies,[1] which gives a few details about him. But it is best to show first how the eighteenth-century debate went. The obvious starting-point is Addison.

He was intent to show Milton's place in the epic tradition of Homer and Virgil; but it is clear from the way in which he rebukes 'ignorant readers' that there were people who thought that similes ought to be as relevant as possible. Milton, says Addison,

> never quits his Simile till it rises to some very great Idea, which is often foreign to the Occasion that gave Birth to it. The Resemblance does not, perhaps, last above a Line or two, but the Poet runs on with the Hint, till has raised out of it some glorious Image or Sentiment. . . . Those, who are acquainted with *Homer*'s and *Virgil*'s Way of Writing, cannot but be pleased with this kind of Structure in *Milton*'s Similitudes. I am the more particular on this Head, because ignorant Readers, who have formed their Taste upon the quaint Similes, and little Turns of Wit, which are so much in Vogue among modern Poets, cannot relish these Beauties which are of a much higher Nature, and are therefore apt to censure *Milton*'s Comparisons, in which they do not see any surprising Points of Likeness.[2]

And Addison, evidently under some feeling of strain, quotes Boileau, who had said: 'Comparisons . . . in Odes and Epic Poems are not introduced only to illustrate and embellish the Discourse, but to amuse and relax the Mind of the Reader,

[1] Vet. A 4 e. 1700.

[2] *The Spectator*, No. 303 (16 Feb. 1712).

by frequently disengaging him from too painful an Attention to the principal Subject, and by leading him into other agreeable Images. . . . It is not necessary in Poetry for the Points of the Comparison to correspond with one another exactly, but that a general Resemblance is sufficient, and that too much Nicety in this Particular savours of the Rhetorician and Epigrammatist.'

Here Addison, with Boileau's help, formulated the orthodox defence of these 'long-tailed comparisons' in a way which is still acceptable to many. Yet a modern reader might be tempted to grant that such similes are common in Homer and Virgil, but that those poets are great in spite of them rather than because of them. They may be a traditional part of the epic, but there are such things as poor traditions. But perhaps it is best to avoid both these positions, and to find both Addison and such a modern reader wrong—Addison for not granting that relevance is better than irrelevance, the modern reader for supposing that what is less good is necessarily bad. There are certainly some similes in *Paradise Lost* which seem to me to have a very limited relevance, but none of them seems bad, merely less good than others. Dr. Johnson's remarks about the invocations are relevant: 'The short digressions at the beginning of the third, seventh, and ninth books might doubtless be spared; but superfluities so beautiful who would take away? or who does not wish that the author of the *Iliad* had gratified succeeding ages with a little knowledge of himself? Perhaps no passages are more frequently or more attentively read than those extrinsick paragraphs; and, since the end of poetry is pleasure, that cannot be unpoetical with which all are pleased.' Many people now believe that these invocations are in some degree integrated with the poem—but what if they weren't? And one might equally ask of the similes, 'superfluities so beautiful who would take away?'[1]

But two other points are relevant to Addison and Boileau. The first is to notice the superb phrasing: 'disengaging him

[1] *Lives of the Poets*, ed. Hill, i. 175.

from too painful an attention to the principal subject'—a cat-like care which anticipates Mr. Eliot's praise for Milton's 'happy introduction of so much extraneous matter' and his 'skill in extending a period by introducing imagery which tends to distract us from the real subject'.[1] The second point is to notice that there was at any rate a part of Addison's mind which hankered for, or at least admired, 'surprising points of likeness'. So he very shrewdly picks out the *ignis fatuus* simile (ix. 633), and praises it as 'not only very beautiful, but the closest of any in the whole Poem. . . . These several Particulars are all of them wrought into the following Similitude.'[2] This was to be a common attitude to Milton's similes; to say that they weren't strictly relevant and that this didn't matter at all—but then to point with pleasure at a simile of strict relevance. Newton, for instance, did not deplore digression, but he exclaimed at the vulture simile (iii. 431): 'This simile is very apposite and lively, and corresponds exactly in all the particulars.'[3] Similarly, Henry Pemberton in 1738 disagreed with the restricting notion that 'the description of the subject brought for comparison should be extended no farther than those very circumstances, wherein it corresponded with the subject, to which it refers'. But he too admitted that 'those similies indeed have a peculiar grace, where the circumstances drawn out to corroborate the description, improve the resemblance'.[4]

Addison's deferential point of view was supported by Pearce, who (with a defensive air) said that, in his similes Milton 'often takes the liberty of wandring into some unresembling Circumstances'.[5] And Richardson agreed jocularly: 'The Main Business being done, the Poet gives the rein a little to Fancy, Entertaining his Reader with what is not Otherwise to the Purpose.'[6]

But ranged against Addison's acquiescence were, first,

[1] See p. 6 above.

[2] *The Spectator*, No. 351 (12 Apr. 1712).

[3] i. 195.

[4] *Observations on Poetry* (1738), pp. 141–2; quoted by H. T. Swedenberg, Jr., in *The Theory of the Epic in England 1650–1800* (1944), p. 366.

[5] pp. 66–67.

[6] p. cl; also pp. 114, 126.

those who thought Milton's 'liberty' licence. So Joseph Trapp in 1715 said bluntly: 'If I must give my Opinion of those *luxurious Comparisons* that deviate from the Subject, which *Homer*, chiefly, among the Ancients, and *Milton*, among the Moderns, run into; I must confess, they neither deserve Commendation, nor are capable of Defence.'[1] And 'A Gentleman of Oxford' in 1756 agreed: '*Milton* is here guilty of one of his common Faults of running away from his *Simile*, whose Beauty consists in its Brevity as much as in any particular Part of its Construction, to make a Parade of his Knowledge of foreign Countries.'[2]

These two sides of the dispute agreed that the similes get off the point, but disagreed as to whether this mattered. So it is the third point of view which is nearest to the twentieth-century one: that usually the details of Milton's similes are subtly relevant. Voltaire in 1727 made a protest: ' 'Tis strange that *Homer* is commended by the Criticks for his comparing *Ajax* to an Ass pelted away with Stones by some Children, *Ulysses* to a Pudding, the Council-board of *Priam* to Grashoppers: 'Tis strange, I say, that they defend so clamourously those Similes tho' never so foreign to the Purpose, and will not allow the natural Reflexions, the noble Digressions of *Milton* tho' never so closely link'd to the Subject.'[3] But this only takes us half-way; on this showing the similes are both 'noble digressions' and 'closely linked to the subject'. It is Falconer's *Essay on Milton's Imitations of the Ancients* that takes the necessary stride forward.

One of the best examples is his association of the Vallombrosa simile (I. 301–4) with similar passages in Homer and Virgil: 'But Milton's Comparison is by far the exactest; for it not only expresses a Multitude, as the above of Homer and Virgil, but also the Posture and Situation of the Angels. Their lying confusedly in Heaps, covered with the Lake, is finely represented by this Image of the Leaves in the Brooks.

[1] *Lectures on Poetry* (tr. 1742), p. 138. [2] *A New Version of P.L.*, p. 46.

[3] *An Essay upon the Civil Wars of France, and also upon the Epic Poetry of the European Nations*, p. 112.

Moreover, the falling of a Shower of Leaves from the Trees, in a Storm of Wind, very well represents the Dejection of the Angels from their former Celestial Mansions; and *their faded Splendor wan* [IV. 870], is finely expressed by the paleness and witheredness of the Leaves.'[1] That seems to me outstanding Miltonic criticism, and its date is 1741.

Nor is it an isolated example—Falconer comments with equal delicacy and imagination elsewhere:

> Thir Glory witherd. As when Heavens Fire
> Hath scath'd the Forrest Oaks, or Mountain Pines,
> With singed top their stately growth though bare
> Stands on the blasted Heath. (I. 612–15)

'This is also a very beautiful and close Simile, it represents the majestick Stature, and withered Glory of the Angels; and the last with great Propriety, since their Lustre was impaired by Thunder, as well as that of the Trees in the Simile: And besides, the blasted Heath gives us some Idea of that singed burning Soil, on which the Angels were standing. Homer and Virgil frequently use Comparisons from Trees, to express the Stature, or falling of a *Hero*, but none of them are applied with such Variety and Propriety of Circumstances as this of Milton; which, tho' it be but one Image, yet contains four Similes; for every Likeness or Point of Comparison is a Simile. I am far from thinking this Closeness in Similitudes a modern Improvement; since, in the best Ancients, we have the finest Examples of it, excepting our Author.'[2]

Here, indeed, we may give added weight to Falconer's criticism when we find that it would not have surprised Milton's first editor—Hume said: 'Their tall Trunks, their vast high Bodies, a Noble Comparison of the Angelick Armies, to the tall Sons of Earth, the Mountain Pines . . . And of their blasted Beauties and faded Glory to their singed Crowns.'[3]

A final instance from Falconer: his remarks on the simile of the bees (I. 768–75), with their 'Straw-built Cittadel' and

[1] p. 23. [2] pp. 24–25. [3] p. 40.

their 'State affairs'. 'Milton has here finely imitated Homer's Simile, and improved it with the Addition of the three last Lines,

> . . . *Or on the smoothed Plank*, &c.

which gives the greater Closeness to his Simile, as alluding to the following Council: The Swarms and Clusters of the Bees, finely express the straitned Croud of the Angels; and the Mention of their rustling Wings, gives it another Propriety which Homer wants.'[1]

The best of the eighteenth-century criticism, then, once more anticipates the subtleties of a modern critic. Of course it is still necessary to curb one's wanton imagination. One of the most famous and beautiful of the allusions will illustrate this: no earthly beauties could compare with Paradise,

> Not that faire field
> Of Enna, where Proserpin gathring flours
> Her self a fairer Floure by gloomie Dis
> Was gatherd, which cost Ceres all that pain
> To seek her through the world . . . (IV. 268–72)

Few would disagree with Mr. Lewis: Paradise is compared to 'Enna—one beautiful landscape to another. But, of course, the deeper value of the simile lies in the resemblance which is not explicitly noted as a resemblance at all, the fact that in both these places the young and the beautiful while gathering flowers was ravished by a dark power risen up from the underworld.'[2] But the further details must not be distorted. What are we to do with 'which cost Ceres all that pain'? It has been suggested that we are to think of Christ. But in that case, the precise correspondence must surely be thought to give way to a looser suggestiveness. Ceres cannot be Christ, in the sense in which Eve is Proserpin; the most obvious thing is that the sexes are wrong, and the correspondence would be intolerable in any case, since Eve is herself later explicitly compared to Ceres. Surely the most that one should say is that Ceres' pain does perhaps suggest the terrible pain

[1] p. 26. [2] *A Preface*, p. 42.

that comes into the world after the Fall, and that the conjunction of this with the word 'cost' perhaps suggests—though it does not state—the suffering of Christ. But it is important to see how very different are the degrees of correspondence.

The same principle can be applied to the similes. Mr. Lerner firmly and skilfully brings out how relevant are the details in the simile that compares Satan's leading of Eve to the tree, with an *ignis fatuus* (IX. 633–42). Almost every phrase reverberates with what we know about Eve and her danger. But even here not every word can be convincingly applied, and when Mr. Lerner[1] sees the words *Pond or Poole* as 'holding in them a distant suggestion of the flood', I think that he himself is acting the will-of-the-wisp. Surely the phrase doesn't hold such a suggestion, or—if it does—it must be the worst attempt ever made to suggest (however distantly) the flood. We have only to put 'Pond or Poole' near Milton's own description of the grandeur and terror of the flood to see how hopelessly inadequate, or mistaken, such an idea is:

all dwellings else
Flood overwhelmd, and them with all thir pomp
Deep under water rould; Sea cover'd Sea,
Sea without shoar . . . (XI. 743–6)

But Mr. Lerner has a total success with another of the similes, Satan as a vulture (III. 431–9), which Newton picked out: 'this simile is very apposite and lively, and corresponds exactly in all the particulars'. Satan the vulture—and we are to remember this when we meet Death later as a vulture—has come from the land of the Tartars (suggesting Tartarus), and is flying towards 'the Springs of Ganges or Hydaspes', the fertile streams of Paradise. He is in search of his prey, 'Lambs or yeanling Kids'—just as when Satan leaps into Eden, he is a wolf after the flock. But he breaks his journey, and Milton makes the relevance of the simile (and of the Limbo of Fools) quite explicit:

[1] *E. in C.* (1954), iv. 306.

But in his way lights on the barren plaines
Of Sericana, where Chineses drive
With Sails and Wind thir canie Waggons light:
So on this windie Sea of Land, the Fiend
Walk'd up and down alone bent on his prey . . .

The correspondences are astonishingly precise— astonishing not only in their precision, but also in the fact that the exactness has not killed the imaginative life of the lines. But even here we have to use our common sense and say 'thus far, and no farther'. It is no use asking what is the narrative equivalent to the Chineses—there isn't one. But this simile is obviously useful to offer to anyone who holds to the 'traditional' idea of the similes as epic ones that pleasantly drift away. Since if we want to reject the correspondences, which can be done only by calling them coincidences, we are accepting not just one coincidence, but five or six. And then, for once, the improbable position is not that of the ingenious explicator, but of the sturdy commonsensical traditionalist.

Unfortunately there is—as Mr. Whaler saw—one factor which disconcertingly complicates any discussion of the relevance of the similes. Namely, that Milton does sometimes use similes and allusions with a clear sense of the fact that they don't fit exactly, that he does sometimes use an unlikeness between the things compared. It was just this that De Quincey acutely fastened on.[1] The trouble here is obvious: that we now have to hand a gambit like 'heads I win, tails you lose'. If a simile does turn out to be relevant, then that is good; and if it turns out not to be, then that is good too, since it is 'ironic disparity'. This is admittedly troublesome, but Milton is a subtly complicated poet; and there seems no doubt that his mind did sometimes work in this way.

Satan from the Limbo of Fools looks up at the palace gate of Heaven:

The Stairs were such as whereon Jacob saw
Angels ascending and descending, bands
Of Guardians bright, when he from Esau fled

[1] See p. 15 above.

To Padan-Aram in the field of Luz,
Dreaming by night under the open Skie,
And waking cri'd, This is the Gate of Heav'n.
Each Stair mysteriously was meant, nor stood
There alwaies, but drawn up to Heav'n somtimes . . .
The Stairs were then let down, whether to dare
The Fiend by easie ascent, or aggravate
His sad exclusion from the dores of Bliss. (III. 510–25)

Here Satan is compared to Jacob when he too saw the gate of Heaven. And the alternatives are inexorable: either Milton is interested in the gigantic differences between Satan and Jacob, or he is not. If he is not interested, then to devote more than five lines to Jacob is strangely wasteful. Surely the length of the allusion and its beauty—

Dreaming by night under the open Skie,
And waking cri'd, This is the Gate of Heav'n—

surely these press us into thinking that Milton was concerned more than casually with Jacob. And his point here is a simple though implicit one: Satan as he sees the gate of Heaven is compared to Jacob doing likewise—but with what different effects, in what different situations; Satan is the arch-enemy of God, Jacob was the chosen hand of God. If a contrast of this kind is not present, then we ought to deprecate the passage (however beautiful), since it would seem to suggest either that Satan was good, or that Jacob was bad. The length and power of the allusion forces us to choose between damaging irrelevance, or likeness turning grimly into disparity.

My own view is that the disparity is meant to be recognized; and that the lines are similar in intention to those which tell how Satan with his spear calls up his shattered troops from the lake, and which compare him to Moses calling up the locusts:

As when the potent Rod
Of Amrams Son in Egypts evill day

Wav'd round the Coast, up call'd a pitchy cloud
Of Locusts, warping on the Eastern Wind,
That ore the Realm of impious Pharaoh hung
Like Night, and darken'd all the Land of Nile:
So numberless were those bad Angels seen . . . (I. 338–44)

The relevance of the locusts is obvious; the evil of Egypt follows the account of 'Busiris and his Memphian Chivalrie'; and Milton brings out the piety of Moses by stressing the impiety of his adversary. Is it possible then to think that Milton was not making deliberate use, not only of the similarity of Satan and Moses at this point, but also of the hideous differences between them? Satan, as so often, is a hideous parody of the good.[1]

But we must remember that we have here a dangerously useful weapon. So let me, before turning to a simile which is arguably of such a kind, take first of all one where it seems that nothing can justifiably find the details relevant. Satan, having been caught in Paradise, is hemmed round by the angelic guard:

as thick as when a field
Of Ceres ripe for harvest waving bends
Her bearded Grove of ears, which way the wind
Swayes them; the careful Plowman doubting stands
Least on the threshing floore his hopeful sheaves
Prove chaff. (IV. 980–5)

Bentley left out the ploughman sentence: 'The Editor deserts the notion, and from a salutary Gale of Wind, . . . he passes to a Tempest, and frightens the Husbandman with the loss of all his Grain. What an Injury is this to the prior Comparison? What are Sheaves bound up in a Barn to the Phalanx, that hem'd *Satan*? Where's the least Similitude?'[2] Mr. Empson commented gleefully: 'It certainly makes the angels look weak. If God the sower is the ploughman, then he is anxious;

[1] Newton commented on X. 409: 'Satan encourages Sin and Death in much the same words as Moses does Joshua. Deut. xxxi. 7, 8' (ii. 244).

[2] p. 143.

another hint that he is not omnipotent. If the labouring Satan is the ploughman he is only anxious for a moment, and he is the natural ruler or owner of the good angels.'[1] Mr. Empson is jubilant, since this allows him either way to make the poem pro-Satan and anti-God. But it seems more likely that here we do have one of the epic similes, beautiful but digressive.

Yet most of them are not of that kind. One of the finest similes in the poem describes Satan as he watches Eve:

> As one who long in populous City pent,
> Where Houses thick and Sewers annoy the Aire,
> Forth issuing on a Summers Morn to breathe
> Among the pleasant Villages and Farmes
> Adjoynd, from each thing met conceaves delight,
> The smell of Grain, or tedded Grass, or Kine,
> Or Dairie, each rural sight, each rural sound;
> If chance with Nymphlike step fair Virgin pass,
> What pleasing seemd, for her now pleases more,
> She most, and in her looks summs all Delight.
> Such Pleasure took the Serpent to behold
> This Flourie Plat, the sweet recess of Eve
> Thus earlie, thus alone . . . (IX. 445–57)

The correspondences are brilliantly close, until we suddenly exclaim with Mr. Whaler, 'But how different is his purpose in leaving the city from Satan's in quitting Hell!'[2] For a moment, Satan has become the simply delighted spectator of rural beauty, 'of enmitie disarm'd, / Of guile, of hate, of envie, of revenge'. Yet it can be only for a moment, and we realize that a *but* will bring back the true Satan:

> But the hot Hell that alwayes in him burnes,
> Though in mid Heav'n, soon ended his delight,
> And tortures him now more, the more he sees
> Of pleasure not for him ordain'd: then soon
> Fierce hate he recollects, and all his thoughts
> Of mischief, gratulating, thus excites.
> Thoughts, whither have ye led me, with what sweet
> Compulsion thus transported to forget

[1] *Some Versions*, p. 172.

[2] *P.M.L.A.* (1931), xlvi. 1061.

What hither brought us, hate, not love, nor hope
Of Paradise for Hell, hope here to taste
Of pleasure, but all pleasure to destroy . . . (IX. 467–77)

And in those superb lines, Satan dissociates himself from the city-dweller, who *is* shown as having come for love, not hate, in hope of Paradise for Hell, to taste of pleasure. All in all, this—which is surely one of the greatest similes in the poem—makes it clear that we cannot do without a sense of disparity as well as of similarity in Milton's similes.

Not that this dilemma is rare in reading poetry. The choice between a dangerous irrelevance and finding directions out by indirections is often forced on us. Emily Dickinson says that

Presentiment is that long shadow on the lawn
Indicative that suns go down;
The notice to the startled grass
That darkness is about to pass.

If this is straightforward, then it is silly; in other words, if we suppose that similitude, and nothing but similitude, is the poem's wish, then we cannot but be disappointed by the similitude's extreme weakness. Presentiment is a sentiment, a feeling; yet here it is symbolized in a moment in nature which is *not* felt by the equivalent of man; the lawn does not feel that the long shadow means the going down of the sun; the grass is not startled and does not feel that darkness is about to pass. If Emily Dickinson was really trying to find in nature an emblem of presentiment, then she failed sadly. But surely she too is fully aware of the fact that there is indeed no emblem in nature for man's presentiments. That is just the point she wants to make, and the impossibility of 'the startled grass' brings home more sharply than ever how different from nature man is, unique in looking before and after. That man is unique, is cause for both dignity and alarm. As W. H. Auden has written,

Happy the hare at morning, for she cannot read
The Hunter's waking thoughts, lucky the leaf

> Unable to predict the fall, lucky indeed
> The rampant suffering suffocating jelly
> Burgeoning in pools, lapping the grits of the desert,
> But what shall man do, who can whistle tunes by heart,
> Knows to the bar when death shall cut him short
> like the cry of the shearwater
> What can he do but defend himself from his knowledge?

But such presentiments, such anticipations, are very much to Milton's purpose in *Paradise Lost*. 'Lucky the leaf unable to predict the fall', but man's unluckiness is also his sense of dignity and of tragedy. Milton's similes very often predict the Fall—and they do so with great variety and subtlety. The same is true of his classical and biblical allusions.

Macaulay has an excellent commentary on the Miltonic style: 'The most striking characteristic of the poetry of Milton is the extreme remoteness of the associations by means of which it acts on the reader. Its effect is produced, not so much by what it expresses, as by what it suggests; not so much by the ideas which it directly conveys, as by other ideas which are connected with them. He electrifies the mind through conductors.'

This is certainly to the point. But unfortunately the examples of the principle at work which Macaulay offered reduce the process to a kind of divine wool-gathering. Of the allusions, for instance, he says: 'A third [name] evokes all the dear classical recollections of childhood, the schoolroom, the dog-eared Virgil, the holiday, and the prize.'[1] This may pass as autobiography, but not as criticism of Milton. To understand the particular moments when Milton 'electrifies the mind through conductors', we do better to turn to the eighteenth century.

It was clear to Richardson that Milton's allusions often merited close and imaginative examination. For one thing, it was Richardson's general belief that 'he Expresses himself So Concisely, Employs Words So Sparingly, that whoever

[1] *Literary and Historical Essays* (1934), pp. 9–11.

will Possess His Ideas must Dig for them, and Oftentimes pretty far below the Surface'.[1] And Richardson was able to put the principle to work in the service of subtle examples. As when the corner of Eden cultivated by Eve is compared to three famous gardens:

> Spot more delicious then those Gardens feign'd
> Or of reviv'd Adonis, or renownd
> Alcinous, host of old Laertes Son,
> Or that, not Mystic, where the Sapient King
> Held dalliance with his faire Egyptian Spouse. (IX. 439–43)

Richardson fastened on *Adonis*: 'The Circumstance of these Gardens of *Adonis* being to Last but a very little while, which even became a Proverb among the Ancients, adds a very Pathetick propriety to the Simile: Still More, as that 'tis not the Whole Garden of *Eden* which is Now spoken of, but that One *Delicious Spot* where *Eve* was, This *Flowrie Plat* and This was of her Own Hand, as those Gardens of *Adonis* were always of the Hands of those *Lovely Damsels*, Less Lovely yet than She.'[2]

This is finely said. Yet the most important of the gardens is the last: that which, not mythical, refers to Solomon and Pharaoh's daughter. Its main purpose is to invoke the beauties of that garden—yet this seems to be very perfunctorily performed, since there is not a word of description. If the beauty of the garden were the sole reason for the allusion, we might be tempted to think that here is epic allusion of the rather empty kind—Milton finding it easier to refer than to create.

But it is significant that the passage which moved Bentley to just such a protest should be the comparison of Paradise and the field of Enna: 'And then, in stead of painting out their several Beauties, as a Pretense for their rivaling Paradise; you give us their bare Names, with some fabulous Story to them, not denoting at all any Beauty.'[3] The answer to this is Mr. Lewis's observation that the real point of the

[1] p. cxliv. [2] p. 416. [3] p. 115 (misnumbered 215).

comparison is that Eve is like Proserpin. And there is the same 'subterranean virtue' in the mention of Solomon's garden. The allusion includes more than beauty: it recalls how a man of great wisdom showed his famous inability to resist a woman. Solomon is a type of Adam, and the allusion has the oblique but powerful purpose of predicting the Fall.

Solomon was traditionally linked with Adam—as at the end of *Sir Gawain and the Green Knight*. Indeed, in Milton's Trinity College manuscripts, one of the entries in the list of subjects for tragedy refers to 'Salomon Gynæcocratomenus', Solomon Woman-governed. Moreover, the account of the heathen gods includes an emphatic mention of

> that uxorious King, whose heart though large,
> Beguil'd by fair Idolatresses, fell
> To Idols foul. (I. 444–6)

Here the aptness to the Fall hardly needs underlining. 'Solomon is "Beguil'd by fair Idolatresses" just as Adam will be by Eve.'[1] Adam, too, was large of heart but uxorious; and he reproaches Eve for beguiling him:

> with the Serpent meeting
> Fool'd and beguil'd, by him thou, I be thee. (x. 879–80)

And Eve is a fair idolatress; after her fall,

> from the Tree her step she turnd,
> But first low Reverence don, as to the power
> That dwelt within. (IX. 834–6)

If the allusion to Solomon in Book I does not reflect on Adam, then there are a strange number of coincidences. That the allusion in Book IX is linked with the earlier one is suggested by the fact that a reference to Adonis follows 'that uxorious King' just as it precedes 'the Sapient King'.

More support can be found in *Paradise Regain'd*. There Satan dismisses the idea of setting women in Christ's eye, not (as one might expect) because the second Adam is stronger than the first, but because he is stronger than

[1] Peter, *A Critique of P.L.*, p. 37.

Solomon. 'Women, when nothing else, beguil'd the heart / Of wisest Solomon'; but 'Solomon he liv'd at ease', and 'he whom we attempt is wiser far / Then Solomon'.[1]

But the verbal points are crucial. 'The Sapient King held dalliance with his faire Egyptian Spouse': twice, Eve is 'his fair Spouse'.[2] Much more importantly, neither *sapient* nor *dalliance* is a common word, and their recurrence together after the Fall (in this same Book) would be a most remarkable coincidence:

in Lust they burne:
Till Adam thus 'gan Eve to dalliance move.
Eve, now I see thou art exact of taste,
And elegant, of Sapience no small part . . . (IX. 1015–18)

At which Adam unfolds the importance of *taste* and *sapience*, combining as they do the two great themes of the poem, knowledge gained by tasting (the Latin *sapere*):

of Sapience no small part,
Since to each meaning savour we apply,
And Palate call judicious . . .

Indeed Eve herself had seen sapience as the great quality of the fruit she had just tasted:

O Sovran, vertuous, precious of all Trees
In Paradise, of operation blest
To Sapience. (IX. 795–7)

The allusion to Solomon, then, ominously and beautifully hints at the Fall. But in that case what of the single-line sentence which follows? It is apparently usually taken as returning us to the serpent watching Eve.[3] But it is also strangely and brilliantly apt *within* the allusion:

where the Sapient King
Held dalliance with his faire Egyptian Spouse.
Much hee the Place admir'd, the Person more.
As one who long in populous City pent . . .

[1] *P.R.*, II. 169–70, 201, 205–6. [2] IV. 742; V. 129.

[3] Editors are silent, but James Paterson in 1744 paraphrased it: '*He*, i.e. *Satan*, admired *Paradise*, but much more *Eve*' (*A Commentary on P.L.*, p. 393).

Is it merely a coincidence that the line is so apt to Solomon and to Adam? That indeed it provides so terse a summary of the whole poem? Adam was struck with wonder by Paradise, 'this happie place'. But he was even more struck by Eve. It is not until the closing lines of the poem that we see the true balancing of person and place, in Eve's moving penitence:

> thou to mee
> Art all things under Heav'n, all places thou. (XII. 617–18)

It is interesting, but no more, that Christopher Pitt's reminiscence of the line should concern Dido and Aeneas, and so be more apt to Solomon than to the serpent:

> Charm'd with his Presence, Dido gaz'd him o'er,
> Admir'd his Fortune much, his Person more.[1]

More relevant is the fact that Adam's sin is twice seen as a matter of too *much admiring* Eve. Raphael, in a very important speech, rebukes him for

> attributing overmuch to things
> Less excellent, as thou thy self perceav'st.
> For what admir'st thou, what transports thee so,
> An outside? fair no doubt . . . (VIII. 565–8)

The conjunction of *much* and *admire* is closer when after the Fall Adam admits that

> I also err'd in overmuch admiring
> What seemd in thee so perfet. (IX. 1178–9)

But there is another way of getting at whether or not it is completely satisfactory to take 'Much hee the Place admir'd, the Person more' as going simply with the lines that follow it. Does Milton ever begin a new sequence of thought with a single-line sentence? Or, more strictly, does he ever use a single-line sentence entirely detached from what precedes it?

Such sentences are rare and emphatic in Milton, because they so obviously conflict with his basic principle of 'the

[1] *An Essay on Virgil's Aeneid, Being a Translation of the First Book* (1728), p. 49.

sense variously drawn out from one Verse into another'. And, as far as I can see, he never uses such a sentence without some continuity with the previous lines.[1]

In other words, if we take this line as simply and solely returning us to the serpent, we are postulating not only a very harsh break (in the work of a poet who is a master of transitions), but also a unique usage of the single-line sentence. Not only is the line extremely apt within the allusion, but Milton's practice would suggest that it belongs there.

Does this mean that the line *cannot* refer to the serpent? It is certainly very apt there too; it fits exactly both with the following simile and narrative, and the fact that it is so often read as belonging to the serpent means that one should not lightly transfer it. In fact, the reasons for treating the line as *within* the allusion are powerful, and so are the more obvious reasons for treating it as *outside*.

But Milton is a master of syntactical fluidity. He achieves some of his finest effects precisely by leaving it possible for a word or a clause to look backward or forward. And what Mr. Prince says of the rhyme-scheme in *Lycidas* could well be applied to Miltonic syntax: 'The rhetoric of rhyme derived from the *canzone* has thus provided Milton with an invaluable instrument—a type of rhyme which looks both back and

[1] Single-line questions, such as 'Who first seduc'd them to that fowl revolt?', are not relevant—in any case they come naturally in a current train of thought, rather than as the start of a new one. Nor are the single-line stage-directions relevant ('Whereto with speedy words th' Archfiend reply'd'). But they too never show a complete break with the previous lines. The continuity is always provided by words like 'whereto', 'to whom', or 'whom thus'. There remain, then, the comparable single-line sentences. Not counting the line under discussion, there seem to be thirteen in *Paradise Lost*. In no case is one of them completely detached from the previous lines. Seven of them, on the contrary, are used to end a speech: 'Awake, arise, or be for ever fall'n' (I. 330. Also III. 735; IX. 566, 732; XI. 180, 633, 835). Three of them are embedded in the continuing argument: 'This was that caution giv'n thee; be advis'd' (V. 523. Also VIII. 490; X. 54). Two show the reciprocation of dialogue—a very different thing from what would be postulated here: Eve 'thus abasht repli'd. / The Serpent me beguil'd and I did eate' (X. 162). And: 'I yeild it just, said Adam, and submit' (XI. 523). The remaining one of the thirteen sentences does, admittedly, begin a new narrative phase, but without snapping the continuity: 'So all was cleard, and to the Field they haste' (V. 136).

forward.' The six-syllable lines 'not only always rhyme with a previous longer line (thus looking back), but they give the impression of a contracted movement which must be compensated by a full movement in the next line (which is always of full length), and they thus look forward. This effect is most marked when, as in most cases, these short lines rhyme with the line immediately preceding them.'[1]

It is at any rate possible that this line is Milton's masterpiece of syntactical fluidity. It stands as a self-contained sentence between two sentences each ten lines long; and it acts as a hinge, with a hinge's property of belonging to both sides, to the preceding allusion and to the following narrative.

> Nature that hateth emptiness,
> Allows of penetration less.

But this would be a supreme feat of penetration, in which two sentences occupy exactly the same space. If this is so—and one should say no more, and no less, than that it may be—then the only way of unfolding the syntax would be to say the line twice:

> Or that, not Mystic, where the Sapient King
> Held dalliance with his faire Egyptian Spouse.
> (Much hee the Place admir'd, the Person more.)
> Much hee the Place admir'd, the Person more.
> As one who long in populous City pent . . .

The modern critical method of tracing patterns of imagery and of cross-reference has been usefully applied to *Paradise Lost*. Naturally the method itself was known to the eighteenth-century commentators. So Richardson[2] placed the right emphasis on Adam's airy lightness of sleep (v. 3–4) by remarking:

> the Sleep of Paradise; in Opposition to
> Grosser Sleep
> Bred of Unkindly Fumes, with Conscious Dreams
> Encumberd (IX. 1049)

[1] *The Italian Element*, pp. 86–87.

[2] p. 192.

But the tracing of these cross-references has proceeded much farther, and has produced some admirable criticism. Mr. B. Rajan[1] illuminated the correspondences between Heaven and Hell; and Milton's full subtlety was brought out by Dr. Broadbent—for example, in tracing the associations of Hell with the chivalric, the technological, and the oriental.[2] Mrs. I. G. MacCaffrey demonstrated how such patterns provide not only a larger unity but also innumerable local felicities. But it was Charles Williams who showed, in one weighty paragraph, just how much feeling and meaning Milton can create in this way:

> At the very end humanity has its turn in the hand again, the hand which has meant so much at certain crises of the poem: at the separation, as if symbolically, of a derived love from its source—
>
> Thus saying, from her husband's hand her hand
> Soft she withdrew;
>
> and in the sin (the derived love working against its human and Divine sources):
>
> So saying, her rash hand in evil hour
> Forth reaching to the fruit, she plucked, she ate;
>
> and so now in the rejoined union of that penitence and humility which Milton knew so well:
>
> They hand in hand with wandering steps and slow
> Through Eden took their solitary way.[3]

That is a very fine piece of criticism, and not least in its willingness to leave much unsaid, its decision not to go remorselessly through the poem listing all the mentions of hands. Not but what the image is potent and frequent. We first see Adam and Eve 'hand in hand', and Milton offers the sacramental form *handed*: 'Handed they went' (IV. 739). Instances crowd in—again and again Milton finds poignancy

[1] *P.L. and the 17th Century Reader* (1947), pp. 44–52.

[2] Hume said of 'their great Sultan': 'The Title of the Turkish Emperours for their Cruelty and Tyrannick Government, well enough apply'd to Satan' (p. 21).

[3] Introduction to *The English Poems of Milton*, p. xix. K. Svendsen amplifies the point—without reference to Williams—through the traditional symbolism of the hands (*Milton and Science*, pp. 111–12).

in this image. But it is not an image that needs an explicator, merely a reminder—as Charles Williams saw.

It is the same with the two other such images: the face, and the flower. It would be easy to go through the poem showing with what variety and pathos Milton brings before us the faces of his characters. Adam exclaims at the fall of Eve:

> How art thou lost, how on a sudden lost,
> Defac't, deflourd, and now to Death devote? (IX. 900–1)

And there rushes into 'defac't' everything that the poem has shown us of sin and its effects: 'A diminution of the majesty of the human countenance, and a conscious degradation of mind.'[1] The passions and pains which scar Adam and Eve and Satan are contrasted with the eternal divine countenance:

> Beyond compare the Son of God was seen
> Most glorious, in him in all his Father shon
> Substantially express'd, and in his face
> Divine compassion visibly appeerd,
> Love without end, and without measure Grace . . . (III. 138–42)

It is not likely to be an accident that 'Grace' there so plangently echoes 'face', nor that the rhyme is proffered by the magnificent chiasmus of the last line—a greater line, perhaps, in this mode than anything that the heroic couplet produced.

'Deflourd', too, draws on those echoes and anticipations which are felt in the blood and felt along the heart of the poem. Eve, the gatherer and guardian of flowers, 'her self, though fairest unsupported Flour', has been deflowered. The felicities which Milton finds in such images are countless. Pope described the comparable miracle in the natural world:

> The spider's touch, how exquisitely fine!
> Feels at each thread, and lives along the line.

It is just this image which comes to mind when we read an eighteenth-century defender of Milton saying that 'he

[1] *De Doctrina Christiana*, Book I, chap. xii; quoted by Stein, *Answerable Style* p. 8.

chose that Subject to place it like a Center to which he might draw as many Lines as his surprising Genius cou'd. The greatest Excellencies of his Poem consist, beyond comparison, more in those Lines than in the Center.'[1]

Sometimes the spider's touch is so fine that it may go unnoticed. Such an example was borrowed by Mr. Empson from the eighteenth century:

> Soon had his crew
> Op'nd into the Hill a spacious wound
> And dig'd out ribs of God. (I. 688–90)

Mr. Empson commented: 'Bentley wanted to read "seeds of gold", but the words here, said Pearce, "allude to the formation of Eve in viii. 463". I call this a profound piece of criticism; "let none admire . . . that soil may best Deserve the precious bane". It is not specially unkind to Eve; to connect her with the architecture of Pandemonium makes her stand for the pride and loyalty that won grandeur even from the fall.'[2]

But it is a pity that, as often, Mr. Empson doesn't show that such a reading, which is beautiful and profound, is also plausible. After all, Hume's straightforward note might be thought enough: 'Continuing the Metaphor of Earths Bowels, he calls the great Hole made in the Hill, *a wide Wound*, and here the Ore, *Ribs of Gold*, almost refined by the Natural Heat of that Infernal Soil.'[3] Not that the continuation of the metaphor contradicts Pearce's suggestion. But why should we believe that there is a hint at Eve? Fortunately, when we look up what Pearce said, we find that his note was slightly, but significantly, fuller than Mr. Empson's quotation: 'I don't doubt but the Poet here by saying, They *open'd into the Hill a spacious wound*, and *dig'd out Ribs of Gold*, alludes to the formation of Eve VIII. 463. he *Open'd my Left, and took from thence a Rib:—wide was the wound.*'[4]

[1] Paul Rolli, *Remarks upon Voltaire's Essay* (1728), p. 61.
[2] *Some Versions*, p. 176. [3] p. 44. [4] p. 43.

Surely the repetition of the 'spacious wound' is important, and it is a pity that Mr. Empson left it out. And Milton takes the rib seriously enough to make it an emblem of Eve's nature:

> all but a Rib
> Crooked by nature, bent, as now appears,
> More to the part sinister from me drawn.[1] (x. 884–6)

Not that we must press the 'ribs of Gold' into anything more than a poignant reminder—the difference between 'rib' and 'ribs' forbids us to see the phrase as more than an enhancing suggestion. Mr. Empson doesn't much bother with verifying his unforgettable insights; but it is necessary if we really are to win back the profound eighteenth-century view of Milton as not only a sublime and gigantic poet, but also a subtle and witty one.

Since the use of these cross-connexions has been well studied recently, I want to comment on only one such image, in an attempt to show that this kind of allusion can radically alter our attitude even to passages usually thought of as laughably bad. Adam and Eve's gardening has often been laughed at; Dr. Tillyard, who calls their work 'ridiculous', has said that 'Adam and Eve are in the hopeless position of Old Age Pensioners enjoying perpetual youth'.[2] At the very least, the gardening is usually thought of as an intractable corner of the myth that Milton could do no more than tidy up.

Certainly he is bound to be involved in many difficulties when he has to show the nature of labour before the Fall. I can think of only one really successful treatment of the paradox, the closing lines of Marvell's 'Bermudas'. The Bermudas were traditionally thought of as Paradise—as Waller said,

[1] In *Milton and Science* (p. 184), K. Svendsen shows that the emblem is traditional, and quotes Joseph Swetnam (1615): 'a ribbe is a crooked thing good for nothing else, and women are crooked by nature'. Arnold Williams provides the relevant context, the commentators on Genesis (*The Common Expositor*, pp. 90–92).

[2] *Milton* (1930), p. 282.

Heaven sure has kept this spot of earth uncursed,
To show how all things were created first.[1]

Marvell's poem describes this Paradise, ending with a brilliantly unobtrusive insight into labour before the Fall:

Thus sung they, in the *English* boat,
An holy and a chearful Note,
And all the way, to guide their Chime,
With falling Oars they kept the time.

In fact, the point is made so unobtrusively that some readers never seem to notice it at all; without any nudge, Marvell tells us that they *rowed* in order to keep time in their song—not, as we would expect in this fallen world, that they sang in order to keep time in their rowing. Before the Fall, man worked simply in order to praise God with 'an holy and a chearful Note'—now life is the other way round. It is a brilliant poetic summing-up of the paradox of pre-lapsarian labour.

It would be foolish to argue that Milton achieves anything like the same success with Adam and Eve's gardening; but he faces very different problems from Marvell. Marvell could rely on a moment of poetic intuition; but Milton is writing a long narrative poem, and the problem cannot be seized once and for all. Yet to me the gardening is far from ridiculous if we are fully aware of what Milton is saying.

This is a case where it is essential to consider, not the separable problem, but the actual words in which Milton presents it. And just as in alluding to the field of Enna, the real focus of the allusion was not on the beauty of the field but on the drama of Eve and Satan, so the gardening is not primarily a matter of horticulture, but is at every point enmeshed with the imminent tragedy.

Let me take Eve's first speech to Adam when she suggests going off on her own:

Adam, well may we labour still to dress
This Garden, still to tend Plant, Herb and Flour,

[1] *The Battle of the Summer Islands*, Canto I.

Our pleasant task enjoy'nd, but till more hands
Aid us, the work under our labour grows,
Luxurious by restraint; what we by day
Lop overgrown, or prune, or prop, or bind,
One night or two with wanton growth derides
Tending to wilde. Thou therefore now advise
Or hear what to my mind first thoughts present,
Let us divide our labours, thou where choice
Leads thee, or where most needs, whether to wind
The Woodbine round this Arbour, or direct
The clasping Ivie where to climb, while I
In yonder Spring of Roses intermixt
With Myrtle, find what to redress till Noon:
For while so near each other thus all day
Our task we choose, what wonder if so near
Looks intervene and smiles, or object new
Casual discourse draw on, which intermits
Our dayes work brought to little, though begun
Early, and th' hour of Supper comes unearn'd. (IX. 205–25)

First, a brief mention of the psychological acuteness here. There is the grave presentation of Eve's self-will, still disguised by words about Adam's superior wisdom and authority (words that do not pause):

Thou therefore now advise
Or hear what to my mind first thoughts present . . .

And subtly making the same point is the contrast between the proliferation of choice for Adam and the direct decision for herself; she doesn't care what he does, and she knows very well what she will do. After all, there follow more than a hundred and fifty lines of argument between them; then she leaves; and when we, and the serpent, next see her, it is exactly where she had insisted she was going when she first mentioned the subject: in the thicket of roses tying up the flowers with myrtle.

But my present concern is not with deft psychology, but with the emblematic correspondences between the gardening and the Fall. The work, says Eve, 'under our labour grows,

/ Luxurious by restraint'. *Luxurious* is before the Fall a harmless horticultural word, but its fallen meaning jostles against it here;[1] luxury is not only one of the most important results of the Fall, it is the first ('in Lust they burne'). And 'luxurious *by restraint*' is also grim with anticipation. Milton at the very beginning of his poem had called on his muse to

> say first what cause
> Mov'd our Grand Parents in that happy State,
> Favour'd of Heav'n so highly, to fall off
> From their Creator, and transgress his Will
> *For one restraint*, Lords of the World besides? (I. 28–32)

Eve's obstinacy is to lead very soon to the Fall, since abandoning the one restraint means abandoning all restraints: 'Greedily she ingorg'd without restraint' (IX. 791).

So that we should be prepared for her words to Adam to tighten from detail to sombre generality:

> what we by day
> Lop overgrown, or prune, or prop, or bind,
> One night or two with wanton growth derides
> Tending to wilde.

'Wanton' begins etymologically as 'undisciplined, disobedient', and ends as 'lustful', so that it compresses the reason for the Fall and the immediate effects of it. Then to describe the garden as 'tending to wilde' finely thrusts home the point. Not that Eve can shuffle off her responsibility, and claim that sin was a natural tendency.[2] But with Eve in it, the garden will certainly tend to wild; so that Adam cries out when he hears that she has fallen—her sin and the thought of losing her shatter the leaves:

> How can I live without thee, how forgoe
> Thy sweet Converse and Love so dearly joyn'd,
> To live again in these wilde Woods forlorn? (IX. 908–10)

[1] On *luxurious* and *wanton*, see pp. 111–12 above.

[2] Mrs. I. G. MacCaffrey: 'the wilderness is there, waiting to encroach at the slightest neglect' (*P.L. as 'Myth'*, p. 154).

There is a similarly subtle hint in the word *redress*: 'find what to redress till Noon'. This is a technical application, to horticulture, of the ancient meaning: 'To set a person or thing upright again; to raise again to an erect position.'[1] But it seems improbable that Milton is unaware of the moral resonance in the word—its moral meaning is also ancient, and found in Chaucer. Eve may believe that she is going to set the plants upright and erect. In fact, she 'her self, though fairest unsupported Flour', will be 'drooping unsustained'. It is a bitter irony that seizes on the word 'redress'.

The poet turns the notes to tragic, too, when Eve says that if she stays near Adam, some *object new* may

> Casual discourse draw on, which intermits
> Our dayes work brought to little.

What in fact is the 'object new' on this fatal day? What but the snake? For as Adam says,

> Reason not impossibly may meet
> Some specious object by the Foe subornd. (IX. 360–1)

And the snake draws on, not casual discourse, but the most pregnant conversation in the history of mankind. There is grim irony, almost parody even, in the echo of God's instructions to Raphael to warn Adam:

> such discourse bring on,
> As may advise him of his happie state,
> Happiness in his power left free to will . . . (V. 233–5)

Casual, moreover, means not only 'which befalls', but also 'which falls', as Milton shows elsewhere in the poem.[2] And the discourse certainly will have *brought* their *day's work to little*.

What is essential, then, is to insist on the huge web of anticipation and echo. So that when Adam in his reply says

> for nothing lovelier can be found
> In woman, then to studie houshold good,
> And good workes in her Husband to promote,

[1] *O.E.D.* 1, from Chaucer on. Examples include the horticultural application—one from Sylvester's Du Bartas.

[2] XI. 562, where 'casual fire' is lightning.

the appropriate comment is not biographical, that Milton is showing his usual 'Turkish contempt of females', but critical—that Adam speaks unwittingly to an Eve who is not exactly going to study household *good*, and who is about to promote in her husband not good works, but the first act of evil.

Milton's demands are very great, and the most important of all is that we should know his poem well enough to be able to see when a phrase, a line, or a moment is touched by tinctures or reflections. His sublimities are superbly direct, but his subtleties depend on our receiving not only the delicacies of simile and allusion, but also those of allusion within the poem itself.

As Milton's earliest commentators saw, his Grand Style is as remarkable for its accurate delicacy as for its power. Miltonic criticism since then, whether hostile or friendly, has tended to dwell most on its power; so that the case for the other virtues has often gone by default. One of the main points to make is that there is more than one 'traditional' way of reading Milton, and that Mr. Empson's choice of the eighteenth-century editors was not capricious or peripheral. Not that the Victorian tradition is wrong. It points to something very important in Milton, but with a dangerously exclusive gesture. His earliest editors were open to more various powers.

But isn't there also something dangerously exclusive in concentrating on Milton's *style* alone? Surely there can be no satisfactory divorce of style from content? In general terms one might reply that for any critical argument to get off the ground, one must reluctantly select from the poem. But certainly the points about the Grand Style ought now to be related briefly to the poem itself.

It seems to me that there is a very close analogy between the successes of the style and the wider successes of the poem. The more closely one looks at the style, the clearer it seems that Milton writes at his very best only when something prevents him from writing with total directness. And the same is true of what is good or bad in *Paradise Lost* in other terms.

Milton's Grand Style is delicately suggestive, very much more flexible or supple than is sometimes thought. To Milton, a man of great conviction, great energy, and great emotion, the danger was of being too direct, of stunning or bludgeoning us. But as Richardson insisted, Milton's felicities 'when they Awaken the Mind do it not with a Sudden Crash, but as with Musick; if they Surprize, they don't Startle Us'.[1] Naturally we are in favour of a poet's words having 'masculine persuasive force'—but masculinity is not enough. At its very best, Milton's style is remarkable for its simultaneous combination of what is energetically strong with what is winning soft and amiably mild. It is this which undoes Mr. Eliot's comparison of Milton's style with Henry James's, since indirectness is to James the congenial excess which directness is to Milton. How often we wish that Milton would not affirm too directly and powerfully. And how often we long for an affirmation of some kind from James.

This is not to say that either in style or in content Milton is never successful in directness. But as a rule it seems that his greatest effects are produced when he is compelled to be oblique as well as direct. The analogy with the wider successes of the poem is clear. For example, it seems to me that there are two descriptions of Paradise which soar above all Milton's other accounts of it; and what they have in common is that neither directly confronts Paradise. The first begins:

> Not that faire field
> Of Enna, where Proserpin gathring flours
> Her self a fairer Floure by gloomie Dis
> Was gatherd . . . (IV. 268–71)

It is, I believe, the very fact that Milton's gaze is *not* directly on Paradise which makes these lines among the most haunting he ever wrote. And the *not* of 'Not that faire field . . .' is

[1] p. cli.

itself an opportunity for Milton to release his full feelings while still gaining all the advantages of the oblique. It seems to me similarly remarkable that if asked to point to the most moving account of Eve in the poem, it is once again these lines that I would quote. Eve is never more powerfully and tragically herself than when Milton glimpses her as Proserpin. Mr. Empson, in the notes to one of his poems, points out that 'a star just too faint to be seen directly can still be seen out of the corners of your eyes'; and his poem itself emphasizes the limited reach of 'the stoutest heart's best direct yell', while at the same time wryly defining the right kind of indirection:

> the spry arts
> Can keep a steady hold on the controls
> By seeming to evade.

The other outstanding description of Paradise seems to me this:

> then shall this Mount
> Of Paradise by might of Waves be moovd
> Out of his place, pushd by the horned floud,
> With all his verdure spoil'd, and Trees adrift
> Down the great River to the op'ning Gulf,
> And there take root an Iland salt and bare,
> The haunt of Seales and Orcs, and Sea-mews clang.
> (XI. 825–31)

Nowhere else in the poem, not even at the magnificent moments when Milton lavishes his full luxuriance on the Garden, do we so yearn for Paradise. And of all Milton's touching oxymorons, perhaps the greatest is the title of his epic.

The finest successes of the poem in larger terms all seem to me to have been created when total directness was impossible. Hell is more memorable than Heaven, because Hell resists directness. Not that it gets out of hand, or that Milton is lax with it; merely that, at any rate in the first two books, its inhabitants are irreducible. Pandæmonium is both beautiful and desperate. In the content of the poem, as well as in its style, Milton is at his best when his directness is at one with indirections. The vibrant understanding which we occasionally feel when we see Satan or Adam and Eve is due to the fact that here Milton is grappling with things that strength alone will not be able to open, things that need delicacy too. A balance that is not precarious and is the result of a strength manifesting itself in innumerable tiny, significant, internal movements—this is the balance of Milton's Grand Style.

Index of the principal passages discussed

Index

PRINTED IN GREAT BRITAIN
AT THE UNIVERSITY PRESS, OXFORD
BY VIVIAN RIDLER
PRINTER TO THE UNIVERSITY